THE ATLANTIC CRITICAL STUDIES

WILLIAM SHAKESPEARE'S

A Midsummer Night's Dream

RATRI RAY

ATLANTIC

PUBLISHERS & DISTRIBUTORS (P) LTD

Published by

ATLANTIC

PUBLISHERS & DISTRIBUTORS (P) LTD

B-2, Vishal Enclave, Opp. Rajouri Garden,
New Delhi-110027
Phones : +91-11-25413460, 25429987, 25466842

Sales Office
7/22, Ansari Road, Darya Ganj,
New Delhi-110002
Phones : +91-11-23273880, 23275880, 23280451
Fax : +91-11-23285873
web : www.atlanticbooks.com
e-mail : info@atlanticbooks.com

Chennai Branch
5, Nallathambi Street, Wallajah Road,
Chennai-600002
Phones : +91-44-64611085, 32413319
e-mail : chennai@atlanticbooks.com

Printed in India
at Nice Printing Press, Delhi

General Preface

The Atlantic Critical Studies are study-aids modelled on the study-aids available in England and America, among other places, and are primarily meant for the students of English Literature of Indian universities.

However, in consideration of the local conditions and the various constraints under which our students have to study—non-availability of relevant critical books, dearth of foreign and Indian journals, inaccessibility to good, well-equipped libraries, just to mention a few of them—the models have been considerably improved upon, both qualitatively and quantitatively.

Thus, while these studies are meant to be comprehensive and self-sufficient, the distinguished scholars who have prepared these study materials, have taken special care to combine lucidity and profundity in their treatment of the texts.

The Select Bibliography at the end is meant not only to acknowledge the sources used but also to help a student in the pursuit of further studies if s/he wants to.

Atlantic Publishers and Distributors (P) Ltd., believe in quality and excellence. These studies will only reconfirm it.

MOHIT K. RAY
Chief Editor [English Literature]
Atlantic Publishers & Distributors (P) Ltd.,
New Delhi

Contents

1

Introduction

It is often thought that the greatness of a genius is recognized only posthumously, and further, he generally lives in poverty. This idea, though, generally true does not hold true in the case of Shakespeare. He, indeed is recognized today for what he was—a powerful dramatist who produced works of unparallelled excellence not only in the sphere of drama, but in other forms also, such is songs, sonnets or narrative poems. His own, contemporaries literary artists as well as the play-going public, recognized and acclaimed his supremacy. The plays were highly successful on the stage, so that he could buy a share in the company that performed them and also bought land and house in his birthplace, Stratford-upon-Avon. He died one of the most prosperous men of his town. This is proof enough of the way in which he was accorded fame and wealth in his own lifetime.

Life-expectation was less in those days than it now is, and according to his own time Shakespeare lived to fairly long age. During the few years of his productivity he produced a wealth of plays, poems and sonnets that has not been equalled by any of his contemporaries. There were many rules and conventions that he had to follow. Sometimes he did follow them (as in The Tempest) and at other times he wrote with a sovereign disregard for them and produced works that stood the test of time. The many different elements of a play, i.e. the plot, the art of characterization, etc., all blend to produce a bouquet of surpassing excellence. The more one reads his plays, the more they grow on him. Words like "sublimity", "universality", "exemplastic imagination", etc., succeed in catching but one or two feathers of this unique phoenix.

He excelled in whatever genre he took up, and within the field of drama itself there is a surprising range and variety. He has written plays of all kinds—tragedies, comedies as well as chronicle plays, and in this he stands alone. Marlow who, had he lived, could have been his greatest rival, wrote only tragedies and Ben Jonson was specialized mainly only in satiric comedies. Tragedy, comedy and chronicles-within these three main genres of contemporary plays, again, there is more variety in Shakespeare than in any poet else. All the four main kinds of tragedy can be found in his works. Marlowe wrote only Conqueror tragedies and Shakespeare, among others, wrote *Macbeth*. Kyd wrote Revenge tragedies, which is represented by *Hamlet* Likewise, the Villain tragedy is to be found in Richard and the Domestic tragedy in *Romeo and Juliet*. Among comedies we have the Romantic comedy (*Twelfth Night*), Pastoral comedies (*As You like It*), Problem comedies (*Measure for Measure*) and Romances (*The Tempest*). One should, moreover, keep in mind the fact that Shakespeare's plays are far too complex to be contained within one label. He took up a popular genre, experimented with it, and took it far beyond its boundaries.

In all (excluding the farce *Merry Wives of Windsor*, he wrote sixteen comedies. They are divided, as given below, into four categories:

(1) The Early Comedies: *The Two Gentlemen of Verona*, *The Comedy of Errors*, *Love's Labour's Lost*, *A Mid-summer Night's Dream.*

(2) The Golden Comedies: *The Merchant of Venice*, *Much Ado about Nothing*, *As You Like It*, *Twelfth Night.*

(3) The Problem Comedies: *Measure for Measure*, *Troilus and Cressida*, *All's Well That Ends Well*, *Timon of Athens.*

(4) The Last Romances: *Pericles*, *Cymbeline*, *The Winter's Tale*, *The Tempest.*

Apart from these, as has already been noted above, he wrote a farce at Queen Elizabeth's express order, *The Merry Wives of Windsor*.

Shakespeare's career began with comedies, and ended also with them, as far as drama is concerned. This will become clear in the brief notes given below of his works (Vide Chapter 3, infra). It is usually thought that comedy means a play that ends happily, with the marriage of the hero and the heroine. This is a rather superficial view. Comedy essentially signifies the triumph of good over evil. The French critic Henri Fluchere has pointed out this basic feature:

> What has always appealed to him with constant tenacity is the haunting sense of order and equilibrium which can be attained only by crushing the forces, of evil by the triumph of the good.[1]

REFERENCES

1. Fluchere, Henri, *Shakespeare*, London, Longmans, Green & Co., 1953, p. 264.

2

The Background

(A) THE SOCIO-POLITICAL BACKGROUND

No literary artist can be completely isolated from his background, and Shakespeare was as integrally connected with his background as anyone else. G.M. Trevelyan says with authority:

> His works could never have been produced in any other period than those late Elizabethan and early Jacobean times in which it was his luck to live. He could not have written as he did if the men and women among whom his days were passed had been other than they were.[1]

Before one starts studying the work of any writer, therefore, it is necessary to know the socio-political background of his time. Shakespeare's life spans a most eventful time in the history of England—the end of the sixteenth and the beginning of the seventeenth century. Here a brief chronological table from the time of the Queen's succession to the throne of England to the death of our poet is given below. It contains the main political, social and religious events of his time.

A Chronological Table 1558-1616

1558 — Queen Mary I dies, Elizabeth I succeeds.

— Mary Queen of the Scots marries the French Dauphin.

1559 — Mary Queen of the Scots declares herself the Queen of England. The Franco-Spanish war ends.

— Church of England re-established more firmly.

1560 — The Scottish Parliament establishes the Reformed Church and breaks with Rome.

1561 — Mary Queen of the Scots returns from France.

— She clashes with the Calvinists.

1562 — The Huguenots begin emigrating from France to England.

1563 — Bubonic plague in Europe.

1564 — **Shakespeare born**. The war between France and England ends.

— England at war with Spain.

— Galileo born.

— The Thirty-nine Articles adopted by the Church of England. Queen Elizabeth tries to enforce uniformity of religion.

1567 — Mary Queen of the Scots abdicates. Rugby Chapel founded.

1568 — Mary Queen of the Scots flees to England and is held captive by Queen Elizabeth.

1569 — Rebellion of the Roman Catholic earls crushed.

1570 — Pope Pius V excommunicates Queen Elizabeth.

1574 — Burbage gets license for the first theatre in London.

1576 — Tycho Brahe begins his astronomical studies.

— Burbage opens the first theatre in London.

1577 — Treaty with the Dutch signed. Sir Francis Drake begins his circumnavigation of the world.

1580 — Sir Francis Drake completes circumnavigation.

1581 — Conversion to Roman Catholicism declared to be a treasonable act.

— Galileo discovers the Law of the Pendulum.

1583 — Plot against the Queen.

— Humphrey Gilbert takes possession of Newfound land for England.

1584 — Sir Walter Raleigh discovers Virginia and names and colonizes it.

1586 — England wins the battle of Zutphen in which Sir Philip Sidney dies.

— Plot against the Queen. Mary Queen of the Scots convicted of treason.

1587 — Rose Theatre built by Henslowe.

1588 — Defeat of the Spanish Armada by Drake.

1589 — Galileo publishes the results of his experiments with falling bodies.

1592 — John Davis discovers the Falkland Islands.

1593 — Absence from the Church on Sundays made punishable by law.

1595 — Southwell, the poet, executed for celebrating Mass.

1596 — England, France and Netherlands form an alliance against Spain.

1597 — Irish rebellion.

— Statutory provisions made for Poor Relief.

— Beggary made illegal.

1598 — The Bodleian Library begun. Globe Theatre opened.

1603 — Queen Elizabeth dies. King James I on the throne.

1604 — Peace with Spain achieved by the King.

— Acts against priests and recusants. Anglican canons made, and enforced.

1605 — Repression of Puritans and Catholics Gunpowder plot.

1608 — Failure of plan for union with Scotland.

1610 — Judicial decision against royal proclamations.

1611 — Parliament dissolved.

1612 — Alliance with German Protestant princes.

— Witches hanged at Lancashire.

1616 — *Shakespeare dies.*

This table presents a fairly clear picture of the contemporary socio-political situation. At the time when Shakespeare was born, the throne of England was in a highly unstable condition. There were plots against the Queen at home and constant warfare with the neighbouring nations abroad. It took the

Queen a fair number of years to establish herself firmly on the throne and bring political stability to England. She was a tolerant ruler as far as religion was concerned and, slowly but steadily she brought a much-needed peace and prosperity to the country. She was :

> to her subjects the symbol of their unity, prosperity, and freedon.[2]

Even religious controversies, chiefly among the Catholics and the Protestants, came to an end. G.M. Trevelyan has declared that the establishing of a definite religion on England was one of her greatest achievements. Her religious policy came to prosper as it reached the very heart of the English attitude:

> ... an attitude to religion that is not primarily Catholic or Protestant, Puritan or Anglican, but which evades dogma and lives broadly in the spirit.[3]

It was a time of expansion in every field. So far as the social hierarchy was concerned, the class barriers did exist, but it was not something that gave rise to resentment anywhere. The feudal lords, were, by and large conscientious, and did not suppress the lower classes. There was, in addition constant changes in the classes and also between them; as G.M. Trevelyan points out:

> Class division, recognised without fuss on either side, were no rigid and were not strictly hereditary. Individuals and families moved out of one class into another by acquisition or loss of property, or by simple change of occupation. There is no impassable barrier.[4]

Each individual was entitled to a fair wage earned by honest labour. This in turn led to a sense of self-respect as well as to self-reliance. There were no bond-men, nor were there slaves. If there was hard work, there was payment for it.

Another important feature of this time was the innovation in the industrial field. The factory system had been made into a new measure of efficiency and the capitalist owner took pride in his productivity. Mining also expanded correspondingly so that many metals like lead, copper, tin and iron became easily available.

National pride reached a pinnacle of glory when Sir Francis Drake succeeded in two famous ventures—the defeat of the Spanish Armada and the circumnavigation of the world. This later feat took, as will be seen in the chronological table given above, nearly three years. A sense of pride and joy pervaded entire England, reflected by the literature of the time.

Another social movement was the colonising movement. King James made peace with Spain in the very first year of his reign. This made the seas safe and settlers started crossing the seas to colonise the newly-acquired foreign lands like Virginia, New England, etc. Hakluyt's work was of influence:

> Hakluyt, in narrating the deeds of our explorers and seamen, directed across the ocean the thoughts of adventurous youths, of scholars, statesmen and merchants, and of all who had money to invest.[5]

(B) THE LITERARY BACKGROUND

Not for nothing is the Elizabethan Age known as the Golden Age of England. The age was prosperous from the socio-political as well as from the literary point of view. A chronological table of the main literary events of the time is given below. It begins with the first performance (not the publication, which is given later) of *Ralph Roister Doister*, ten year before Shakespeare was born. His own plays are not mentioned here.

A Chronological Table 1554-1616

1554 — Sir Philip Sidney and Lyly born.
— *Ralph Roister Doister Staged.*

1557 — Tottel's *Miscellany.*

1558 — Kyd, Greene, Peele, Lodge born.

1561 — Bacon born, *Gorboduc* performed.

1563 — Drayton and Donne born.

1564 — Shakespeare and Marlowe born.

1565 — Norton and Sackville's *Gorboduc.*

1566 — *Supposes* by Gascoigne, Udall's *Ralph Roister Doister.*

1567 — Campion and Nashe born.

1575 — Heywood and Tourneur born.

— *Appius and Virginia, Gammer Gurton's Needle.*

1576 — *Paradyse of Daynty Devises.*

1577 — Holinshed's *Chronicles.*

1579 — *Shepheardes Calendar* by Spenser.

1585 — Kyd's *The Spanish Tragedy.*

1586 — Sir Philip Sidney died. Lyly's *Endimion.*

1587 — Marlowe's *Tamburlaine*, Lyly's *Gallathea.*

1589 — Marlowe's *Jew of Malta.*

1590 — *The Faerie Queene,* Bks, I-III published.

1591 — *Astrophel and Stella*, Daniel's *To Delia.*

1592 — Revised *Arcadia, Arden of Feversham.*

1595 — *Amoretti, Epithalamion, Apologie for Poetry.*

1598 — Marlowe's *Hero and Leander.*

1599 — Spenser dies.

1600 — *England's Helicon, Cynthia's Revels.*

1601 — Dekker and Marston's *Satiromastix, Jonson's Poetaster.*

1603 — Dowland's *Third Book of Songs, Sejanus, Woman Killed with Kindness, The Dutch Courtezan.*

1604 — Chapman's *Bussy D'Ambois*, Marston's *Malcontent.*

1605 — Drayton's *Collected Poems*, Middleton's *A Trick to Catch the Old One.*

1606 — Lyly dies. *Yorkshire Tragedy*, Jonson's *Volpone,* Tourneur's *The Revenger's Tragedy.*

1607 — Beaumont and Fletcher's *Knight of the Burning Pestle.*

1608 — Fuller and Milton born.

1609 — Beaumont and Fletcher's *Philaster*, Fulke Greville's *Mustapha.*

1610 — Jonson's *The Alchemist* performed.

1611 — Spensor's *Collected Works, The Authorised Version of the Bible, A King and No King.*

1612 — Crashaw born. Chapman's *Iliad*-I-XXIV, Donne's *The Second Anniversarie,* Webster's *The White Devil.*

1613 — Constable and Overbury die. Samuel Purchas's *Purchas His Pilgrimage.*

1614 — Overbury's *Characters*, Lodge's *Works of Seneca*, Sir Walter Raleigh's *History of the World*, Jonson's *Bartholomew* Fair, Webster's *The Duchess of Malfi.*

1616 — **Shakespeare dies.** Jonson's *Epicene.*

It is a coincidence that the years covering Shakespeare's life, from 1564 to 1616, are the best years of this Elizabethan-cum-Jacobean age. Some historians think that the date can be shifted back to Sidney's birth in 1554 and that is what has been done in the table given above. This was definitely the best time from a literary point of view. In the table above the stress has fallen on poetry and drama, but many important prose works had also been published. Many of the poetical and dramatic works, too, have not been mentioned, for it is not possible to give all the names, so numerous they are.

One must remember that if Sidney had a poor opinion about contemporary drama it was because during his lifetime the best dramatic works had not yet been produced. During Shakespeare's own childhood and adolescence many plays were written and staged, but all of an inferior kind, *Gorboduc*, the only play for which Sidney had a few good words, was more Italian than English. In 1587 a play had been put up for the queen's entertainment and had been specially written for the occasion by a group of eight writers. This play, *The Misfortunes of King Arthur* has only historical value today. Such works cannot come up to what Shakespeare, Marlowe and the others were to write, for, though they have historical importance, they have dramatic value. It would be a few years later that drama will come into its own, to amply justify the opinion generally accepted:

> The characteristic and most distinguished form that literature assumed in renaissance England was drama.[6]

The situation is marginally better in the field of sonnets, songs and narrative poems. The first few books of Spenser's *The*

Fairie Queene and his *Shepheard's Calendar* had already been published before Shakespeare wrote his *Venus* and *Adonis*, his first narrative poem. The sonnets of the Earls of Wyatt and of Surrey had been published by Tottel in his famous *Miscellany* and it was in the last decade of the century that the famous sonnet-sequences started to be written. Three of them have been mentioned in the table given above; Sidney *Astrophel and Stella*, *Daniel's To Delia* and Spenser's *Amoretti*. From 1680 onwards the countless love-songs started to be written. The poets were mostly anonymous and are known today under the appellation of "the Elizabethan nest of singing-birds." Some of these collections have been included in the table above, like *The Paradyse* of *Daynty Devises*, *England's Helicon*, etc. There are many songs in Shakespeare in which their influence can be traced. The main theme of the songs, as of the sonnet-sequences, is love, but love of a light-hearted kind:

> The song-lyric, as developed in accord with the musical art of the time, is too light an instrument to utter the deeper notes of passion, and its theme is fanciful love, love that laughs and entreats and sings from the very blitheness of soul.[7]

The Elizabethan Age poured forth a dazzling stream of many kinds of poems. Prose was also flourishing in the hands of writers like Bacon, Sir Thomas Browne, Burton, Hooker and others. Our immediate concern, however, is drama.

Kyd's famous play *The Spanish Tragedy* was a revenge tragedy in the mode of Seneca. This play became instantly popular and later came to be taken as a model for revenge tragedies. *Tamburlaine*, with which *Marlowe* started his meteoric career, rivalled Kyd's in popularity. He had to write a sequel to it, so popular did it become. Burbage, and later Henslowe established theatre halls for the performance of these plays and all the great dramatists honed their skill there. Experiments were being made continually and the five-act form of drama branched out into many directions. Tragedies of four different kinds and comedies catering to different kinds of audiences were produced in abundance. These were supplemented by serious plays like the chronicles, and light works like the farces. Shakespeare, Ben Jonson, Webster, Tourneur, Chapman, Beaumont and Fletcher are some of the great names.

Tragedy followed the lead of Seneca and came to be known as the "blood-and-thunder tragedy." These have been classified into four divisions: the Conqueror tragedy, of the kind that Marlowe wrote, the Revenge tragedy, represented the best by Kyd's play, Villain tragedy like *The Changeling by* Middleton and Rowley, and the Domestic tragedy like the anonymous *Arden* of *Feversham*. The categories are not mutually exclusive and one play can easily have the characteristics of more than one category. Our poet's *Othello* for example, can be labelled as both a villian tragedy and a domestic one.

Comedy, of many different kinds, flourished in the hands of Shakespeare, Ben Jonson and many others. M.C. Bradbrook, dividing Elizabethan society into three sections, has allotted a different kind to each. Society, according to her, was divided into the Court, the Country and the City. Shakespeare's comedies come mostly under the first of these. Within these three main classes there are sub-divisions. Shakespeare's romantic comedies (often known as the Golden comedies), to which *A Midsummer Night's Dream* belongs, are distinctly different from his Dark Comedies, though both were written for courtly audiences. Satirical city comedies were written chiefly by Ben Jonson, Webster, Marston et al., and the two dramatists Beaumont and Fletecher wrote what today are known as tragi-comedies in collaboration with each other.

Apart from these there were numerous farces, providing boisterous enjoyment. Like the satirical comedies, these too usually dealt with characters taken from beyond the aristocratic class. Shakespeare's own *Merry Wives of Windsor* which was specially commissioned by the Queen, was a play of this type.

A special type of dramatic entertainment was the masque. These were very popular and were specially used for celebrating happy occasions like betrothals, weddings etc. Such plays made use of mythical and supernatural characters like nymphs, satyrs, gods, goddesses, fairies, etc. Gorgeous costumes, extraordinary settings, etc., were needed for these productions and naturally they became very expensive. They were used at Court and by the aristocratic households. This is of interest in the present instance because the play under discussion has often been called a masque (*vide* Chapter 4, section b, *infra*). Very often the lords and ladies of the Court themselves acted in these plays. They made use of song and dance and thus provided the element of spectacle as per classical rules. Ben Jonson wrote many such courtly masques, with sets designed by Inigo Jones.

This brief account will scarcely serve to bring home to the student the rich wealth of Elizabethan and Jacobean drama. Above everything else it must be remembered that these plays were all extremely stage-worthy and the writers, actors and directors made their livings out of them. M.C. Bradbrook sums up the position thus:

> Security, stability and easiness had been achieved, and the particular lingusitic problems which vexed the previous generation could not re-occur. The English tongue was now capable of eloquence, and their language was to the generation that followed 'our nation's best glory.'[8]

REFERENCES

1. Trevelyan, G.M., *Illustrated English Social History*, Vol. 2, Harmondsworth, Penguin Book Ltd., 1960, p. 125.
2. *Ibid.,* p. 15.
3. *Ibid.,* pp. 75-76.
4. *Ibid.,* p. 62.
5. *Ibid.,* p. 107.
6. Craig, Hardin, *The Literature of the English Renaissance: 1485-1660*, New York, Collier Books, 1950, p. 71.
7. Carpenter, Frederick Ives, ed., *English Lyric Poetry: 1500-1700*, London, Blackie and Son Ltd., p. 47.
8. Bradbrook, M.C., *The Growth and Structure of Elizabethan Comedy*, London, Chatto and Windus, 1955, p. 41.

3

Life and Works

(A) A SHORT BIOGRAPHY

The biographical details of the Elizabethan writers are rather sketchy and that too, not very dependable. Much of these details, anecdotes and incidents are more legendary than historical. Yet there is such a wealth of biographical material on Shakespeare that many of the dates and a few of the events can be relied upon as historically true. This is not surprising for, during his own lifetime, he came to be acclaimed as a fine dramatist and poet. Irving Ribner points out:

> As a dramatist Shakespeare acquired considerable reputation during his own lifetime. It continued to grow in the centuries following his death in 1616, accumulating as it did so an accretion of legends and anecdotes.[1]

Added to these legends, there are entries made in the village register and other documents. The many biographies of Shakespeare have been based on these. A chronological table of the important events in his life is given below:

A Chronological Table of the Chief Events of his Life

1564 — April 23, the supposed date of birth of Shakespeare.

— April 26, Shakespeare christened at the local parish church of Stratford-upon-Avon.

1571 — Possible time of enrolment in the Grammar School.

1578 — His father suffers severe financial loss.

1582 — Shakespeare gets married to Anne Hathaway.

1583 — Birth of Susannah, his first child.

1585 — The twins, Hamnet and Judith, are baptised.

1586 — Shakespeare's supposed departure for London.

1593 — *Venus and Adonis* published by a fellow villager.

1594 — *Rape of Lucrece* published *Titus Andronicus* staged.

1596 — Death of Hamnet his only son at 12 years.

1597 — Shakespeare buys New Place.

1599 — He buys shares in the Globe Theatre.

1602 — The birth of his first grandchild. He buys one hundred and seven acres of land.

1604 — His company taken under royal patronage and given the name of the King's Men.

1611 — He retires from the company and comes back to settle in his native village.

1613 — *The Tempest* staged. Perhaps he acted in it.

1616 — His Last will and Testament drawn up.

— April 23—Shakespeare dies on his fifty-second birth anniversary.

— April 25—He is buried in the Chancel of Stratford Church.

The exact date of birth is not known, for the register of Baptism recorded the date of baptism, not of birth. The register in the Church of Stratford-upon-Avon records, in official Latin:

1564, April 26, Gulielmus Filius Johannes Shakespeare.[2]

Contemporary custom dictated the baptism of a baby three days after its birth. It is, thus, assumed that he was born on the twenty-third of April, the place being the village of Stratford-upon-Avon and the county Warwickshire. According to the Christian Saints' Calendar, this day was known as St. George's day, who was the patron saint of England.

There are no dependable documents of his childhood but it can be taken for granted that he spent a happy and secure childhood in the bosom of a living and prosperous family. He was the eldest son, so his position in the family was an important one. John Shakespeare, his father, was a prosperous tradesman, much respected in society. Eventually he became the mayor, by which time the little village had expanded into a town. In 1565 his father rose to the position of the highly coveted post of the alderman. By this time he was in a position to claim the status of a gentleman (i.e. the landed gentry as differentiated from a trader). This, in the feudal set-up of the day, carried great importance. On his mother's side, the family was socially higher than that of his father. Mary Arden, his mother, belonged to a family of the small landed gentry.

The countryside around the village was unspoilt as yet by industrialization. The little boy would run wild in the lap of benevolent nature. The memory of this beautiful surrounding was to produce the lovely and lyrical passages of nature description in his plays. *A Midsummer Night's Dream* is specially rich in them.

His father was a Justice of Peace as well as the High Bailiff of Stratford. As such, he had to take active part in judicial matters. As Shakespeare was the eldest son, he often accompanied his father to the law courts and thus gained inside knowledge of legal procedures. The trial scene of *The Merchant of Venice* could not have been so well-written otherwise.

In order to educate the masses, the Queen had established Grammar Schools all over England and Shakespeare was admitted in one. Legends have it that at this time he was about seven and a most reluctant student. His biographers invariably refer to the famous passage in *As You Like It* where he describes the school-boy:

> Then the whining schoolboy, with his satchel
> And shining morning face, creeping like snail
> unwillingly to school.[3]

These schools were named as Grammar Schools, but much more was taught besides grammar. The stress fell on Latin grammar and literature. It is rue that Shakespeare did not get a classical education as boys of the aristocracy did, but he acquired a fair amount of knowledge in the classics in this school. Ben Jonson had laughed at his "Little Latin and less Greek" but he was being unfair. Shakespeare studied in this school till he was about 14 or 16, it is not known for sure which age exactly, nor is it important.

The schools of those days followed a uniform curriculum and uniform hours. They had long hours, starting from six in the morning and going on till five in the evening. There were, however, frequent breaks. There had to be, in all, two and a half hours' break during the day. The curriculum ran thus in all schools.

Poetry: *The Bucolica* of Mantuan.
The Eclogues and *The Aeneid of Virgil.*
The Poems of Horace.
The Metamorphoses of Ovid—The source of his classical references.

Prose: Caesar, Livy, Cicero.

Drama: *Ten Tragedies* of Seneca
The Comedies of Plautus
The Comedies of Terence

Shakespeare, thus, had a solid foundation of classical education. The numerous classical references in the play to be studied (and also in the others) are from first-hand knowledge. One of his biographers has observed in a pertinent manner:

> Today all scholars are agreed that Shakespeare was a well-educated man of his times, that he certainly continued to further his education by wide reading throughout his life and that there is no display of learning in any one of his plays which could not have been acquired at the Stratford Grammar School.[4]

It should also be noted here that the entire idea of his having attended this school has not been accepted by all his biographers. John Dover Wilson raises the objection that as his father was a Catholic, he may not have put Shakespeare in the Grammar School at all. Instead he could easily have put his son in the service of one of the great Catholic noblemen of the time. Shakespeare would have received his education in such a household, and gained an inside knowledge of the lifestyle of the nobility also.

As to how long he continued his studies—this is not known for sure. His father's fortunes seem to have undergone some reversals. He was withdrawn from the school during his teens, perhaps without completing his education. Every year of school-life at this time is of crucial importance, and it cannot be guessed how much this withdrawal had affected his future life.

These years were fruitful in another way, for it was at this time that many travelling companies of players had visited his village. Such itinerant groups were patronised by the great noblemen of the time and were named after them. Thus there were groups belonging to the Earls of Leicester, Warwick and Worcester. They enacted the traditional mediaeval allegorical plays and interludes as well as the modern five-act plays written by the learned in imitation of classical models, like *Gorboduc*, etc.

It was about this time, in his late teens, that Shakespeare's young mind was invaded by love. He fell in love with Anne Hathaway from Shottery, a village a few miles from Stratford. She was the daughter of a prosperous farmer and a girl much sought after, for she was very charming. There is a couplet often quoted by his biographers from an unknown source, testifying her attractiveness:

Anne hathaway, she hath a way
To charm all hearts, Anne Hathaway.

Shakespeare was fortunate enough to win her love. She was eightyears older than him, but this was of no importance to the young lovers. They got married on November 28, 1582. At this time he was not yet nineteen, while she was twenty-six. Their first child, a daughter, was born next year. She was baptised on May 26, 1583, as Susanna. Nothing can be known of their married life—how happy it was or anything else. Nearly two years later the twins, Hamnet and Judith, were born. They were baptised on February 2, 1586. Hamnet died in 1596.

Shakespeare, thus, became a man, though barely twenty-one, beset with the cares of paternity, with a wife eight years older than himself. By this time he had three children to provide for. He must have realized that it was imperative for him to get a job that paid enough for his family to subsist upon.

What exactly he was doing at this time is not definitely known, though there are several anecdotes. John Aubrey, one of the first biographers in English literature, says that he was teaching in a school near his own village. Another anecdote has become so well-known as to be commonly accepted. At Charlecote there was a deer park belonging to Sir Thomas Lucy and it is said that Shakespeare, along with some other young men, stole a deer from there. They got caught and it is thought that Sir Thomas had ordered the young men to be whipped and put into prison. The general opinion is that it was because of this that Shakespeare left Stratford in 1586. A contemporary clergyman and Thomas Betterton the actor, brought this story to the notice of the public but it is to be doubted how true it is.

Another story is also available. It is said that he joined provincial dramatic companies as an actor and spent quite a few years as such. What has given birth to this concept is a will left by a certain wealthy gentleman of Lancashire in which the name of William Shakeshafte has been used, mentioning him as a player in his service. It has been thought that this Shakeshafte is but another name for Shakespeare. Such variants were not at all rare in that time, for English was but newly coming into its own, it was still in a fluid condition as a language.

The group named the Queen's Men visited Stratford at this time and it is thought that this made Shakespeare's thoughts turn towards London. Other troupes also visited the village and thus Shakespeare became familiar with stage performances while still quite young. In 1583 there were three well-known groups which produced plays at Stratford and in 1587 which is probably when he left for London two famous and well-organised troupes had come there. Many of his biographers think that he had not only watched the performances but had acted in them as well. Hamlet's famous conversation with the players gives ample proof of first-hand knowledge of stage-craft, and acting.

The six or seven years from 1586 to 1592 are known as the Dark years, for very little is known about them. Though actual facts are wanting, anecdotes abound. Some say that he had got a job as a prompter's assistant. It is also said that he looked after the horses of the noblemen who rode to the theatre-hall. He had, however, found a fellow townsman named Richard Field. This man had left Stratford a few years before Shakespeare did and had, by this time, become a well-established printer in London. It was this Richard Field who published his *Venus and Adonis* in 1593 and *The Rape of* Lucrece next year, in 1594, to general acclaim.

It is a remarkable coincidence that both Marlowe and Shakespeare arrived at London at the same time. They were born in the same year also, as can be seen by comparing the two Chronological Tables. The decade of the eighties was highly stimulating from many points of view. It was the time when Sir Francis Drake was scouring the Spanish Main and Sir Philip Sidney was writing the first sequence of love-sonnets, *Astrophel and Stella*. His *Arcadia*, also, was perhaps being drafted at the same time. Out there in Ireland, Spenser was composing *The Faerie Queene*. That famous group of young intellectuals, the University Wits, was converging towards London from different places in England. Lyly, its leader, had already produced his *Euphues* and was now turning towards drama. Two of his comedies, *Campaspe* and *Sappho and Phaon* had been performed for the Queen herself by the choir of the chapel Royal in 1584. George Peele had presented his charming musical play *The Arraignment of Paris*. Thomas Kyd, Robert Greene and Thomas Nashe had already arrived at London which was the centre of all contemporary activities, cultural or otherwise. Marlowe's *Tamburlaine* was presented in 1587, by which time our poet was definitely present there. It was a truly wonderful time, with horizons receding further and further in every field. F.E. Halliday says:

> Shakespeare had arrived in London at the most thrilling moment in its history's thrilling, however, not only because danger, anxiety, expectation and hope were in the air, but also because the long awaited dramatic revival was now imminent.[5]

So this was the London to which Shakespeare came. He watched the plays that were being staged, perhaps acting minor parts in them, and went on adding to his store of knowledge all the time. The very first reference to his name is to be found in a work by Greene which is today remembered chiefly for this reason. It is a pamphlet, named *Greene's Groats-worth of Wit Bought with a Million of Repentance*. There occurs a letter at the end of this work in which Greene addresses his friends Peele, Nashe and Marlowe. He warns them against actors and particularly mentions a certain actor in an oblique manner. The reference is definitely to Shakespeare whom he not only ridicules but castigates in no uncertain terms:

> Yes, trust them not: for there is an upstart crow, beautified with our feathers that with his Tyger's heart wrapt in a Player's hyde, supposes he is as well able to bombast out a blank verse as the best of you: and being an absolute Johannes factotum, is in his own conceit the only Shake-scene in a country.[6]

There are two clues here that point to our poet. The line "Tyger's heart wrapt in a player's hyde" is a deliberate distortion of Shakespeare's line "O tiger's heart wrapped in a woman's hide" in *Henry VI, Pt. III*. Next there is the word "Shake-scene" which is a sarcastic reference to Shakespeare. Such a reference is eloquent of spite and professional jealousy. It serves the useful purpose of making us think that by this time Shakespeare had become so important as to be a serious challenge to the others. The University Wits were well-established at this time, yet our poet, young as he was, caused heart-burn and misgivings in them. He must have appeared to these elegant and accomplished men like a half-educated country yokel, so this was no mean achievement for him.

These years are termed as the years of apprenticeship, when he was learning his craft. Yet they were highly productive as well. The sonnets, the two narrative poems, the *Henry VI* trilogy, *Richard III, Titus Andronicus, The Comedy of Errors, The Two Gentlemen of Verona* and *The Taming of the Shrew*, were all written at this time. They were all highly successful, even a play like *Titus Andronicus* which has little literary value. The title-page of this play reveals the fact that it was published in 1594, the text being:

> ... as it was played by the Rt. Hon. the Earl of Derby, the Earl of Pembroke, and the Earl of Sussex their servants.[7]

All the three were well-known companies and the fact that they all put it up in quick succession shows its popularity. The list given above is significant in another way: it means that Shakespeare's talent was not limited to any genre. Kyd and Marlowe wrote only tragedies but Shakespeare, at the very outset of his career, could write successful comedies (*The Two Gentlemen of Verona*), tragedies (*Titus Andronicus*) and histories (*Richard III*) as well. Thus by 1594, when Marlowe had already been killed, Shakespeare had proved his versatility and stage-worthiness.

He had already joined the group known as the Lord Chamberlain's Men by the end of 1594. The fact that he was a valued member of the group can be surmised because his name occurs with those of will Kempe and Burbage in a receipt from the Royal Treasury where all of them had been paid for having produced two plays at Court. Shakespeare continued with this company till the very end.

By this time he was a successful dramatist and it is thought that he paid a visit to Stratford. It was like a joint family, with Shakespeare's father, now in his sixties, as the head. The children, though grown up, were still with the parents. Shakespeare himself was twenty-eight and his children were no longer babes in arms. Susanna was nine and the twins were seven. Hannet thus was old enough to go to school. Shakespeare stayed here for four months and it is thought that he wrote *Richard* III and *Venus and Adonis* during this visit. The poem was dedicated to Henry Wriothesley, the Earl of Southamptom appeared to be the supposed "onlie begetter" of the famous sequence of love-sonnets to be written in near future.

The Earl of Southampton was nearly ten years junior to Shakespeare in age. He became Shakespeare's patron and soon enough a deep friendship developed between them. The sonnets give the impression that there was an intense and loving relationship between the patron and the poet. This may be true or not—there is no way of knowing for sure. These sonnets also describe a Dark Lady who, along with Mr. W.H., to whom some of the sonnets are dedicated betrayed Shakespeare. Mr. W.H. has been identified by some as the young and aristocratic Earl of Southampton and Shakespeare's passionate love for him has been expressed in the best and most intense manner of Courtly Love. The sonnets make one think that Shakespeare's love for Mr. W.H. was an intense and petrarchan love and he was attracted, in a different way, to the Dark Lady. He introduced the dark lady (woman coloured ill) to the friend and two fell in love with each other. This double betrayal devastated the poet:

> Two loves I have, of comfort and despair,
> Which like two spirits do suggest me still;
> The better angel is a man right fair,
> The worser spirit a woman coloured ill.[8]

How much of this harrowing story is true cannot be known for sure, but, though it may be entirely mythical it should be included in any account of his life. It cannot be doubted that Shakespeare had an emotion bordering on idolatry for the Earl. He dedicated not only the sonnets but the two narrative poems also to him and proclaimed his passionate attachment in the dedication to *The Rape of Lucrece*.

Henceforward Shakespeare's life assumed a security that is vitally necessary for an artist. He could afford to buy a share in his own company—the means, it is believed, being supplied by the Earl. A time of literary and financial prosperity ensued:

> That Shakespeare already had sufficient wealth to join in this project would by itself make evident that he was a man of some prosperity.[9]

In those times a poet, unless he had private means, had to have a patron. A life dedicated to the Muse was not always a prosperous one. Whereas his erstwhile enemy Greene was languishing in sickness and poverty, we have Shakespeare buying property:

> It meant all the difference between the dreadful insecurity poor Greene had, and others, died of, and having firm ground under his feet.[10]

The Lord Chamberlain's Men, which is the name his company went under, became the leading theatrical company in London. Before the end of the reign of Queen Elizabeth it gave thirty-two performances in Court alone, apart from public stagings.

It is necessary to understand the literary perspective of this time; only then shall we be able to have a measure of Shakespeare's success. He was the only dramatist to survive the devastation of the Plague. Kyd was already dead at thirty-five years of age, and Marlowe, whom he already thinks of as a rival, died suddenly at a drunken brawl at the age of twenty-nine. Greene was dead at thirty-four. Peele would die in a few years, Lyly and Lodge had virtually stopped writing. Nashe was more interested in turning out pamphlets than plays. Shakespeare had no rival worth the name. Ben Jonson, who was the only dramatist of a calibre like his own, would appear in a few years. At the moment Shakespeare's star was riding high.

The light-hearted early comedies now poured out from his pen. He was enjoying life and literature and it is thought by many biographers that he has produced, as Halliday says, "a half-mocking and unconscious projection of himself" in Lord Berowne of *Love's Labour's Lost*. By now, in 1595, he was of thirty years, fully established in a joyous, successful career. The first literary mention of his name occurs in a poem written at this time by one Henry Willoughby, an Oxford undergraduate. Shakespeare is mentioned as a mentor who gives the poet good advice in matters of the heart and the student also praises his poetry, particularly the narrative poem:

> Yet Tarquin plucked his glistering grape
> And Shakespeare paints poor Lucrece's rape.[11]

In 1597 his only son Hamnet, then eleven, died, and no one was left to carry on the line. Shakespeare was writing *King John* at this time. He had at the desire of his father, pursued the matter of applying at the Heralds' college for the granting of a coat-of-arms. This would give the family the status of a gentleman which, in the feudal-system society of the time, was of great significance. This was granted and Shakespeare came back to London as a gentleman. At this time he also bought New Place, the second best house in Stratford. This little village had grown into a town by this time, and Shakespeare's house was bettered only by the Town Hall.

He had come to be acknowledged as a master dramatist by 1598. In that well-known document of the time *Palladis Tamia* the author Francis Meres waxes eloquent over his works, as here:

> ... the sweet wittie soule of Ovid lives in mellifluous and hony-tongued Shakespeare, witness his *Venus and Adonis*, his *Lucrece*, his sugred sonnets among his friends.[12]

Meres gives a list of the plays that had been written and staged so far. This list is of a great help to scholars in determining the dates of his works. Meres also affirms that Shakespeare is the English Plautus and Seneca in comedy and tragedy.

Shakespeare was accepted as the best dramatist of his time by the enthusiasts of the time, and his company also got a like recognition. In 1603 the Queen passed away and King James VI of Scotland succeeded her as King James I of England. Then the Lord Chamberlain's Men came under royal patronage and was given the name of the King's Men. This was a great honour for now they had become the recognized servants of the King. The men of the company would be given the royal livery to wear. They would appear frequently at Court and take part in all royal pageants and processions.

From now on there are many records of all of Shakespeare's activities. In 1602 he bought a hundred and seven acres of land for farming and later in the same year he bought a cottage and a quarter acre of land. He had continued acting in the plays staged by his company, whether his own or others'. There is a record of how he had acted in Ben Jonson's historical tragedy Sejanus, staged by the King's Men in 1603.

In 1603 there was another epidemic of plague in London and he returned to Stratford. It was at this time that his great tragedies were written. *Hamlet*, which was the last play to have been written in Queen Elizabeth's time, was staged in 1602.

Othello, the first of his Jacobean plays, was performed at Court in 1604. The Chronicles and the problem comedies were also written during this time. It was a time for sombre evaluation of life and person. F.E. Halliday, referring to these works, points out that the Jacobean times brought about a radical change in him:

> ... a change not only of matter, but of manner as well, of the dramatic medium and vehicle of his theme, for the one demanded and necessitated the other, and it is possible to make a broad distinction between his Elizabethan and his Jacobean poetry.[13]

By now Shakespeare was dividing his time almost equally between London and Stratford, spending his summers at home. His first grandchild was born in 1608 and the same year his mother passed away. His time in London was drawing to a close, for he would stay there for three more years only.

He had now started upon his last Romances. The sombre Problem comedies and the anguish of the tragedies lay in the past, the pomp and pageantry of the chronicle plays were also left behind. Instead, Shakespeare had reached the calm waters of true maturity and started creating a serene pastoral world. The sonnet-sequence was published in 1609 and in 1611 (according to Irving Ribner) he retired to Stratford.

Though he had retired, his connections with London were kept up. He continued coming there till the very end of his life. For example, he got the Blackfrair Gate House in 1613. His name continues to appear in many documents. It is also true that he kept up his connections with the stage, for *The Tempest* was performed at the end of 1612 on the occasion of a royal betrothal and it is thought that he himself acted in the role of Prospero, and blessed the couple.

In 1616 his will was drawn up and can still be seen in Somerset House. Two months after this he passed away, on April 23.

His grave was ornamented with rich and complex symbols. There is a bust of himself, quill in hand. There are Corinthian columns on the sides, supporting a cornice. On the cornice there are two allegorical figures symbolising Rest and Labour.

Shakespeare's coat-of-arms (granted by the Herald's College) is placed between the two figures and the entire thing is surmounted by a skull. Under the bust of the poet there is a memorial tablet with a Latin couplet and a sextet in English inscribed on it. The grave bears an epitaph in the form of a quatrain, thought to have been written by the poet himself though one cannot be sure:

> Good friend for Jesus sake forbeare
> To dig the dust enclosed here!
> Blest be the man yt spares these stones,
> And curst be he yt moves my bones.[14]

(B) SHAKESPEARE'S WORKS

Shakespeare's biographers have drawn up a tentative scheme of his dramatic and poetic career. They have based it on the entries made in the Stationer's Register, Henslowe's Diary which recorded the dates of the performances of some of the plays and a few other such sources.

The dates of the performances of many of the plays are not known. The same is the case with the time of composition. Finally, some of the plays (like *Titus Andronicus*) were published quite early and some not. Inspite of many such difficulties, critics are more or less agreed on the following chart.

Phase I

1591 — *The Comedy of Errors.*

1592 — *The Two Gentlemen of Verona, Henry VI, Parts I, II and III.*

1593 — *King Richard III, Romeo and Juliet, Venus and Adonis.*

Phase II

1594 — *The Rape of Lucrece, The Sonnets, Titus Andronicus King Richard II, A Midsummer Night's Dream, Love's Labour's Lost, King John, The Taming of the Shrew.*

1595 — *The Merchant of Venice.*

1597 — *Henry IV, Part I.*

1598 — *Henry IV, Part II, The Merry Wives of Windsor.*

1599 — *King Henry V, Much Ado About Nothing, Julius Caesar.*

1600 — *As You Like It, Twelfth Night.*

Phase III

1602 — *Hamlet, Troilus and Cressida, All's Well that Ends Well.*

1604 — *Measure for Measure, Othello.*

1605 — *King Lear*

1606 — *Macfbeth*

1607 — *Antony and Cleopatra*

1608 — *Coriolanus, Timon of Athens, Pericles.*

Phase IV

1610 — *Cymbeline, The Winter's Tale, Tempest*

1611 — *Henry VIII.*

Shakespeare's career has been roughly divided into the phases given above though they are not by any means mutually exclusive. The different phases often overlap, as for example, some critics would say that the works up till *Love's Labour's Lost* belong to the first phase and some say that *Pericles* belongs to the last phase, not the third. At a rough estimate however, his career can be divided into the four phases given above. The first phase is known as the phase of Experiment, from 1591 to 1594 or perhaps to 1595. This was the time when he was learning his craft by mostly revising and reconstructing plays that were already in existence. During this early period he made occasional use of rhyming and end-stopped lines. This can be seen in *A Midsummer Night's Dream* as well (*vide* Ch. 11, *Poetic Style, infra*). There is much exuberant playing with words, as in *Love's Labour's Lost*. The art of characterization has not developed noticeably.

The second period, that of Development, is from 1594-95 to 1601. The Chronicle plays and the Golden Comedies were written during this time. By now he has attained mastery over the poetic medium, i.e. dramatic blank verse. As far as characterization goes, he has started plumbing the depths of the human mind. The plot are managed in a masterly way.

The third period ended in 1608. There is a remarkable change in mood in the plays of this time. The exuberance of wit, the light-hearted characters have gone. Instead there is sombre contemplation of evil—evil in human nature as well as in Nature. In this he reflects the spirit of the age superlatively well:

> The conflict between good and evil, ugliness and beauty, innocence and crime, purity and impurity, hope and disgust, love and hate, order and disorder, natural laws and the anarchy produced by the passions—all is resolved in Shakespeare's so-called 'dark period' with an infinite despair.[15]

The Great Tragedies and the Problem Comedies also known as the Dark Comedies, belong to this stage.

The last phase, or the Romance period, goes on to 1612 and the last four Romances belong to this time. Here we see a calm and serene Shakespeare, who has reconciled himself to the existence of evil and hands over the future to a younger and purer generation:

> As his career draws to a close Shakespeare turned back to his youth, and his implicit theme is always that of fertility, resurrection, joy of life.[16]

These four plays were succeeded by two more. There was some controversy about *Henry VIII*, but it has now been ascribed to him, and *The Two Noble Kinsmen* is a work of collaboration with Fletcher.

(C) BRIEF NOTES ON HIS WORKS

The Comedy of Errors

The shortest of his plays, many critics take it to be his first. It was performed at Court in 1594 but it is not known whether this was the first staging or not. The plot is taken from Plautus's *The Menaechmi.* He has but one pair of twins in it and Shakespeare has two. So the intrigues, mistaken identities, etc., are doubled. The theme of the relationship between husband and wife, which Shakespeare will take up in *The Taming of the*

Shrew, gains prominence here. The dramatist presents both the sides—that of the husband as well as that of the wife.

The Two Gentlemen of Verona

Critics usually regard this play as the first of his romantic comedies. There are two pairs of lovers, two servants and two fathers, making a symmetrical pattern. The theme is of the conflict between love and friendship, with the emphasis falling on the latter. Along with this there is the theme of forgiveness and reconciliation. This appears in this play for the first time and will go on appearing till in the last plays it dominates the entire work. Many features of his mature comedies are also present, as crossed love, disguised heroines, exile and flight. Julia is a precursor of Rosalind and Portia, just as Silvia foreshadows Juliet and Lance the later jesters.

Henry VI, Parts I, II and III

This trilogy is the first of the Chronicles, which are a class by themselves. No other Elizabethan dramatist wrote so many. He wrote ten of them, including *Henry VIII*. The pomp and pageantry of royalty captivated his imagination. The serious issues of the duties of kings and their human aspects, all fascinated him. The spirit of patriotism cast a glory over everything else—king and country.

The plays were based on the famous *Chronicles* of Raphael Holinshed and staged in 1592. It became so popular that this trilogy was staged three times in eight days. It presents a world of ferocity and betrayal and ends in regicide. Greene had referred to one of its lines.

Richard III

This play belongs more to the genre of tragedy than to chronicles. The *Henry VI* trilogy shows the influence of Marlowe and in this play it is even more intense. The hero, King Richard III, is a Marlovian figure but far more complex than the typical heroes of Marlowe. This play, except for *Hamlet*, is Shakespeare's longest and is very stage-worthy. The figure of the King dominates the entire play and thus his tragic end makes the play more of a tragedy than a history. This is the main difference between this play and the *Henry VI* trilogy.

Many critics tend to group this play with the trilogy and call the whole sequence a tetralogy. As far as the time covered is concerned, this can be done quite easily but usually they are treated separately.

Romeo and Juliet

This play tells one of the most popular stories of the time—a story of family feuds and star-crossed love. As till now, Shakespeare's tragedies are tragedies of Fate, and family feud takes the place of fate. It controls the lives of the two young lovers, placing insuperable difficulties along their way. The kind of hero for whom character is destiny has yet to be formed. This has happened because he has followed the original story very closely in it. Some of the scenes, particularly the Balcony scene, have become classics, to the extent of being parodied. Shakespeare's genius expresses itself, if not through the characters, then through its blank verse, which is of great lyrical beauty. The character of Mercutio is said to be marginally autobiographical.

Venus and Adonis

This is the first of his narrative poems. Based on classical mythology, the story is taken from Ovid. The poem was so successful that it ran through ten or eleven editions in his own life time. Narrative poetry was a new experiment for him, but he had excellent models to guide him, specially Marlowe's *Hero and Leander*. It is so highly sensuous that it can be classed as erotica. He has used a stanza of six lines in it, a quatrain followed by a couplet. It is a pattern highly suitable for narrative poetry, being a smoothly flowing metre and simpler than the Spenserian stanza.

The Rape of Lucrece

This too, like *Venus and Adonis*, is a narrative poem based on classical myths, and, like it, is dedicated to the Earl of Southampton. It is not as light-hearted a poem as the former one for here he explores the feeling of guilt in Tarquin. It is thus a rather sombre poem and these psychological complexities raise it above the level of a merely narrative poem. Tarquin has become a tragic figure. The poet has used the rhyme royal stanza in it; seven iambic pentametre lines rhyming ab ab b c c. He manages this complex from in a masterly manner.

The Sonnets

This sequence of a hundred and fifty-four sonnets is dedicated to Mr. W.H., named as "the onlie begetter". The sonnets, in their intensity of passion as well as their beauty of expression, are unique and supposed to be autobiographical. Out of these hundred and fifty-four sonnets, the first 126 are addressed to Mr. W.H., who is supposed to be Henry Wriothesley, the Earl of Southampton. The remaining twenty-eight are addressed, except for the last three, to the Dark Lady, who was perhaps Mary Fitton, one of the maids of honour of Queen Elizabeth. This is a unique feature, for the sequence is addressed to two persons, one of them a man, whereas the other sonnet-sequences of the time were addressed to just one person, a lady. The sonnets explore the relationships involved in such a triangular situation, very intensely.

Titus Andronicus

This falls within the genre of Revenge Tragedies and is also the first of the Roman tragedies. As such, it is a typical blood-and-thunder tragedy and follows Kyd's *The Spanish Tragedy*. It contains a parody of one of the most famous passages of Kyd. It was highly popular at the time (*vide* Shakespeare's life, *supra*).

Richard II

Shakespeare's plays do not, usually, have much topical relevance, but this play is an exception. Ireland was posing a great problem and this is the theme of the play. It reflects the political situation of the time so well that the Queen had become extremely angry on seeing it. "I am Richard II, know ye that?" She had exclaimed, "This tragedy is played forty times in open streets and houses." The play shows the deposition of King Richard II. This was such a sensitive issue that the deposition-scene had to be omitted when the play was staged. The character of Richard II is supposed to be a study in weakness and has been depicted with great sympathy. Shakespeare shows himself to be able already to handle characters in a most delicate manner.

A Midsummer Night's Dream

The best of the early plays, this is the work which is going to be studied. It has been a popular work from the very beginning, with adults as well as schoolchildren, particularly because of the supernatural element in it, as in *The Tempest.*

Love's Labour's Lost

Produced in 1594, this play is brilliant for its sparkling dialogues, specially those of Lord Berowne and Lady Rosaline. There are four pairs of courtly lovers and a few humble characters have also been brought in. Lord Berowne, the wittiest of the lords is supposed to be slightly autobiographical. He, in a famous passage renounces flowery diction:

> Taffeta phrases, silken terms precise
> Three-piled hyperboles, spruce affectations
> Figures pedantical: those summer flies
> Have blown me full of maggot ostentation
> I do forswear them.[17]

This marks a significant development in the poet's dramatic career.

King John

Though this play is an entirely historical one, yet it has contemporary relevance as well in an indirect manner. Shakespeare, as a rule, avoided the controversial issue of religion, yet in this play he has taken it up. It is the only such play. King John had carried on a life-long struggle with the Roman Catholic Church and the supremacy of the Pope. Queen Elizabeth had done the same, to the extent that she was excommunicated by the Pope (*vide* Ch. 2. Socio-Political Background, *supra*). It is not, however, a religious play but a patriotic one and foreign policy is the central theme.

The Taming of the Shrew

Many critics hold that this is the first of his plays to have an Italian setting. It was performed in 1594. Though an early play, the two main characters are strongly delineated. Katharine, the Shrew of the title and Petruchio the tamer, are both strong, credible characters. The main theme is the relationship between husband and wife and the conflict for supremacy between them. This was a very valid theme for the audience of his day. In all it is a rollicking play, highly stage-worthy. Shakespeare has created another female character as foil for the shrew, which throws both the characters into relief.

The Merchant of Venice

The great age of the Golden Comedies starts with this play. The merchant after whom the play is named is Antonio, but he cannot claim the title of the hero. This is because the position of the most important character has to be given to Shylock who is the villain of the piece. He is a class by himself. The heroine Portia is one of the most important female characters Shakespeare has created. The Elizabethan convention of disguises is used most effectively in this play for each one of the three female characters adopt disguises, though for short durations only. His poetic style has reached a high standard of excellence. There is solemn, thoughtful poetry in the mercy-speech and lyrically beautiful poetry in the moonlight scene.

Henry IV—Part 1 and 2

The English Chronicle play reached its highest point in these two plays. Falstaff whom Queen Elizabeth called "the fat knight" is the main attraction of the play. His rejection by King Henry V is one of the most moving scenes. The rejection, however, is fully justified, for that part of his life has come to an end. King Henry V cannot roister about with Sir John the way Prince Hal did. The play is about the duties and responsibilities of kingship and the King has to shoulder his burdens. The first part with the amusing doings of Falstaff, is entertaining, but the second part is of more psychological interest. But Falstaff remains immortal. Everything might be forgotten, but Falstaff is remembered as one of the greatest comic figures ever created.

The Merry Wives of Windsor

This play was specially ordered for by the Queen. She liked Sir John Falstaff so much that she wanted a play to be written about "the fat knight in love". The play is hilarious and begins at the point where Sir John was left at the end of *Henry IV*, Part. 2. The play, otherwise unimportant, gains special significance because it is thought that Shakespeare had poked fun at Ben Jonson's humour characters. This is said particularly with corporal hym in mind, who makes an inordinate use of the word "humour" in every second sentence he speaks in the play.

King Henry V

This play presents the dramatist's concept of the ideal King. There are two main themes that rule the play—kingship and patriotism. Shakespeare presents the positive as well as the negative side of war—bravery and endurance on one hand, and death and destruction on the other. King Henry, the boisterous Prince Hal of the earlier plays, is presented as the ideal king, with all the qualities necessary for leadership. The historical triumph at Agincourt is shown in a vivid and graphic manner, with Henry V manifesting himself as a strict but just king. Falstaff goes to Arthur's bosom in this play, a-babbling of green fields.

Much Ado About Nothing

This is the second of Shakespeare's four Golden Comedies. It is double-plotted, and the theme is love. This theme, too, is treated in two different ways. There is physical love based on appearances which in this case prove to be deceptive. The Hero-Claudio plot takes up this aspect of love and the Benedick-Beatrice plot takes up the theme of the rejection of married love which makes its appearance again and again in the works. His craftsmanship shows itself to better advantage than in *The Merchant of Venice*, for here the main plot is easily differentiable from the sub-plot. As in the other romantic comedies the lovers move towards a higher consciousness of love and responsibly, integrating themselves within the framework of society.

Julius Caesar

This Roman Tragedy is definitely the most political play of Shakespeare. The plot has little comedy in it. The central theme is the opposition between tyranny and liberty. Characterisation shows itself in the creations of persons who project themselves as living, three-dimensional individuals. The play is eminently stage-worthy, specially the Forum Scene. Lord North's translation of Plutarch's *Lives* supplied the story and Shakespeare shows his economy and resourcefulness by adapting many of the prose passages in this book into appropriate blank verse. He makes use of the supernatural element by introducing the Ghost of Caesar.

As You Like It

This is acknowledged to be the cheeriest and the sunniest of the Romantic Comedies. The major part of the play is located in the Forest of Arden. There are four pairs of lovers, taken from different levels of society and illustrating different types of love. They are all neatly paired off in the end. There is the courtly love of Rosalind and Orlando, as well as the more down-to-earth love of the shepherds. One of the most charming heroines of Shakespeare, Rosalind, enlivens the play with her wit. The convention of disguise and mistaken identity plays a prominent part in the play as the two heroines are in disguise in most of the scenes. The famous passage about the seven stages of man as well as the equally famous lyric 'Under the green wood tree' occurs in this play.

Twelfth Night

This is the fourth and the last of his Golden Comedies. It contains all the usual ingredients of popular comedies like disguises, mistaken identities, the separation and unions of siblings, etc. Plot-structure presents the usual features—a main plot with courtly love and aristocratic characters and a comic sub-plot. Sir Toby is a diluted version of Falstaff and Malvolio is a puritan melancholic. He was extremely popular with the audience. This play presents one of the most important Fools or court jesters in Shakespeare. Feste is highly accomplished and in dramatic importance is second only to the Fool in *King Lear*. The disguise-convention has been used to provide much entertainment.

Hamlet

This is perhaps the best-known play of Shakespeare. It is the first of the four Great Tragedies. It follows the basic pattern of a revenge tragedy but the character of the hero, Hamlet, that like a giant, dominates the play to such an extent that the other features of the play are often neglected. He is today looked upon not as just a hero with the flaw of indecision in his nature, but also as a typical intellectual. Shakespeare shows us that the crude blood-and-thunder tragedy of Kyd can be sublimated to such an extent that the limitations of the revenge tragedy are left far behind and the play becomes a sophisticated play with the quality of true sublimity and universality.

Troilus and Cressida

The Problem Comedies of Shakespeare all present a highly serious treatment of the seamy side of life and human nature and tremble on the verge of tragedy. This play is as close to a satire as Shakespeare ever came. It gives a satirical view of the themes of love and war. Ulysses is a character who is said to come very close to the poet.

All's Well That Ends Well

This too, like the foregoing one is a Problem Comedy. The basic theme is the conflict between virtue and nobility as in the Bertram-Helena plot, but there are several sub-themes, i.e. the conflict between old and young generations. Shakespeare shows himself far less able to endure the follies and vices of humanity as the difference between the braggart soldier Parolles and Falstaff clearly illustrates.

Measure For Measure

This too, like the two problem comedies preceding it, is a sombre play. Paradoxically enough it is the only other play, besides *As You Like It*, to have four marriages in it. Forcing a man to marriage by trickery which was present in *All's Well* also makes its appearance here. The sole ruler of a country withdraws from the state after having appointed a deputy and comes back to observe the state of affairs in disguise. This is an old theme and along with it goes the theme of justice, which is a recurring theme in these later plays. This play contains the famous song "Take O take those lips away" about which A.E. Housman had said that it was nonsense, but ravishing poetry.

Othello

This is Shakespeare's first Jacobean play, as *Hamlet* is the last of his Elizabethan Tragedies. It has been labelled as the

Romeo and Juliet of his later phase and is a study in jealousy Othello and King Leontes in *The Winter's Tale* are both studies in jealousy but the outcome is tragic here and otherwise in the later play. The character of Iago, about whom Coleridge has used the famous phrase "motiveless malignity" is one of the unforgettable villains of Shakespeare. Desdemona the heroine is one of the most pathetic creations of the poet. As the play affects a limited family circle, it has been classified as a domestic tragedy and insofar as the tragedy is the result of the plottings of Iago it is a villain tragedy.

King Lear

This play now vies for the place of the greatest of his tragedies with *Hamlet*. It has been called a Cosmic drama, showing man's place in the universe. The story is taken from several sources, like the old play of *King Leir*, *The Mirror for Magistrates* and Sir Philip Sidney*'s Arcadia*. The poet has woven all these diverse strands together to produce a unique play of elemental passions. A primitive legend is transformed into a terrible tragedy that, nonetheless, has the quality of universality. The word which is usually applied to it is "sublime." The character of the Fool is unique. He is not only the wisest Fool but also serves many other complex purposes. The play has been compared with Dante's *The Divine Comedy*.

Macbeth

This is the darkest of the tragedies, a play of gloom and horror. Shakespeare was paying a tribute to the Scottish King by choosing a story from Scottish history. He has given the unique character of Lady Macheth and has made use of the supernatural element in many different ways in this play.

Antony and Cleopatra

This Roman Tragedy forms a sequel to *Julius Caesar*, though it is entirely different in theme. Here the theme of love predominates. The unforgettable character of Cleopatra dominates the play. The play is so complex that critics cannot decide whether to call it a history, a symphony, a political play or a tragedy.

Coriolanus

This is the last of the tragedies, a political and a Roman Tragedy. So it is usually grouped with the two other Romans tragedies. The hero's noble nature is in conflict with society. He hates the populace and this brings tragic doom on him, for he is rejected by the mob and joins the enemy, to bring ruin upon his country and himself.

Timon of Athens

This is not a finished product and for that very reason affords insights into the poet's creative processes. The play ends with the hero's withdrawal from society, yet there is a sense of its being an unfinished work. This is usually classed as a problem comedy.

Pericles, Cymbeline, The Winter's Tale, and The Tempest

This quartet of plays is known as the Last Romances and in all of them the theme is the same. Sin and repentance leading to forgiveness, and the tainted older generation giving way to a purer new generation. *The Tempest* is the last play of Shakespeare and Prospero's renunciation of magic is thought to be the poet's farewell to the theatre.

Henry VIII

The authorship of this play had been disputed for a long time but now it is attributed to Shakespeare. It is a history play, but ends with the assurance of the continuity of life, as the last Romances do. It is a study on the theme of patience in adversity. Not only does the King learn patience, but so do the others.

The Two Noble Kinsmen

This is a dramatization of *The Knight's Tale* in Chaucer's *Canterbury Tales* and is a collaboration with Fletcher. Shakespeare wrote the major parts of Act I and part of Act III and V. When, however, Fletcher brought in a rather vulgar sub-plot Shakespeare left off collaboration. He did not write any other work in collaboration with others, as many of his contemporaries had done.

REFERENCES

1. Ribner, Irving, *William Shakespeare: Life, Times and Theatre*, London, John Wiley & Sons Inc., 1969, p. 31.
2. Cited in Halliday, F.E., *The Life of Shakespeare*. London, Gerald Duckworth and Co. Ltd., 1961, p. 20.
3. *As You Like It*. Act II, scene vii, II. 145-147, p. 38. Ware, Wordsworth Classics, 1993.
4. Ribner, I., *Op. cit.*, pp. 38-39.
5. Halliday, F.E., *The Life of Shakespeare*, London, Gerald Duckworth & Co. Ltd., 1961, p. 60.
6. Quoted in Ribner, I., *Op. cit.* p. 45.
7. Quoted in Rowse, A.L., *William Shakespeare: A Biography*, London, Macmillan & Co. Ltd., 1963, p. 100.
8. Booth, Stephen, ed., *Shakespeare's Sonnets*, New Haven and London, Yale Univ. Press. 1977, p. 123 (Sonnet No. 144).
9. Ribner, I., *Op. cit.*, pp. 50-51.
10. Rowse, A.L., *Op. cit.* p. 201.
11. Halliday, E. *Op. cit.*, p. 118.
12. *Ibid.*, p. 138, Ribner *Op. cit.*, p. 52.
13. *Ibid.*, p. 183.
14. Quoted in Ribner, *Op. cit.*, p. 64, as well as by many others.
15. Fluchère, H., *Shakespeare*, London, Longmans Green & Co., 1953, p. 54.
16. *Ibid.*, p. 265.
17. *The Illustrated Stratford Shakespeare*, London, Chancellor Press, 1982, p. 164. All quotations from Shakespeare, unless otherwise specified, will be from this text.

4

The Story and the Genre

(A) A BRIEF OUTLINE

Shakespeare goes back to the pagan times in this play for it takes place at the time when Theseus, one of the great heroes of classical mythology was the king of Athens. It was a time which was half-savage, for at that time there was a law in Athens which was typical of a strictly patriarchal society in which the male head of the family was all-powerful. This law decreed that a father had the right to marry his daughter to the man of his own choice or condemn her to death. Egeus the father of Hermia wants his daughter to marry Demetrius but she wants to marry Lysander for they love each other whereas Demetrius's love for her is one-sided. As, according to the old Athenian law, Egeus can condemn his daughter to death, he claims this privilege from Duke Thesues who cannot deny it to him.

Though Theseus cannot go against the rule, he can yet mitigate it by offering Hermia the option of living as a priestess. In despair Hermia and Lysander decide to elope. They fix the next night for this elopement. First they will leave Athens separately and meet in the forest nearby. Then they will go to the house of Lysander's aunt which is seven leagues away from Athens. The cruel Athenian law is not at force there and the lovers will be free to marry there.

They confide this plan to Helena, their childhood friend. This girl is in love with Demetrius who, however, loves Hermia. Helena is so deeply in love with him that she is ready to do anything to win his approval. She at once goes and tells him of the projected elopement of the lovers so that he will be grateful to her.

Though disaster threatens the pair of lovers, yet for the kingdom itself it is a time for festivities, for the Duke is going to marry in four days' time. Hippoyta, the queen of the Amazons, is his bride and she has already come to Athens for the wedding. The very opening lines of the play give us this in information. Theseus says:

> Now, fair Hippolyta, our nuptial hour
> Draws on apace: four happy days bring in
> Another moon: but O, methinks how slow
> This old moon wanes![1]

Everyone in the kingdom is anticipating a time of festive gaiety and a group of humble artisans decide to celebrate the royal wedding by presenting a play to the King and the Queen. The group comprises Quince the carpenter, Bottom the weaver, Flute the bellows-mender, Snout the tinker, Snug the joiner and Starveling the tailor. These six 'mechanicals' as Shakespeare himself describes them, decide to go to the forest to rehearse their play in privacy and secrecy. The play they have chosen to put up is the story of Pyramus and Thisby which is actually, a tragic story and most unsuitable for celebrating a wedding. All six of them, however, are so ignorant that they do not realise this inappropriateness. This group of six characters provide comic relief and Shakespeare presents them with good-humoured tolerance, not satirically.

Then, in due time the lovers Lysander and Hermia meet in the forest the next night. Demetrius, followed by Helena has also come there in search of the lovers. The six mechanicals have also come to the forest. Thus, very early in the play, the dramatist has made the noble as well as the humble characters converge to the forest where the main action is going to take place.

The four young people and the six comic characters, however, are not the only ones in the forest, for the forest has its own denizens. This wonderful forest is the natural habitat of a completely different set of characters—the fairies. There are three main fairy characters and four servitors, besides a few others. Oberon is the king of the fairies and Titania is their queen. Puck or Robin Goodfellow is the special servant of Oberon. The king and the queen are at outs with each other for they both want the same boy (a human one) as their page. At present it is Titania who has got the boy. She knows that Oberon also wants him and she will not give him up.

Seeing that she is adamant in her resolve, Oberon decides to get the boy by a trick. He sends Puck to fetch the juice of a certain flower which, put on the eyelids of Titania when she is asleep, will make her fall in love with the creature she first sees on waking up. Her husband will make her surrender the boy to him before undoing this magic. While he is waiting for Puck to fetch the juice he sees Demetrius and Helena. Seeing how Helena loves Demetrius but is not loved in return, he directs Puck to put some of the juice upon Demetrius's eyes in such a way that he will fall in love with Helena. Puck has not seen them.

So far as Titania is concerned the plan goes well. She falls asleep and Oberon puts a few drops of the juice on her eyelids. The person she sees first on waking up is Bottom, the weaver. Unfortunately Puck has mischievously put an ass's head on him and Titania falls in love with this ass-headed Bottom.

The plan goes awry with the Athenians. Lysander and Hermia feel tired and fall asleep and Puck drips the love-juice on Lysander's eyelids, for he takes them to be the pair of lovers Oberon had described. It must be remembered that Puck had not seen Demetrius and Helena just as Oberon had not seen Lysander and Hermia. It so happens that Helena reaches the place just as Lysander awakes and he promptly falls in love with her. Now the position of the lovers becomes very complicated. Hermia loves Lysander who loves Helena, and Helena loves Demetrius who loves, Hermia. All this is seen by Oberon and Puck. In order to undo the mistake, Oberon drops the juice on the eyelids of Demetrius who, on waking up, sees Helena and falls in love with her. So now both the men are in love with Helena. All this, again, is seen by Oberon and Puck. Oberon thinks that Puck, who is very mischievous, has done this deliberately to bring all these mishaps about.

> This is the negligence. Still thou mistakest,
> Or else commit thy knaveries wilfully.[2]

He then plans out a future course of action which will unravel all this tangle. Puck, who being a fairy, is invisible, pretends to speak with Demetrius's voice to Lysander, challenges him to fight and lures him on into the darkness of the forest. He then speaks to Demetrius with Lysander's voice and lures him on too, thus separating the two young men. Both of them are tired by now and lie down to sleep. Then Helena lies down near Demetrius and falls asleep. Hermia falls asleep near Lysander. Now the fairies take a hand for the last time in human affairs. Puck drops the juice upon Lysander's eyelids and goes away.

Meanwhile, Oberon comes to Titania and Bottom, both of whom are asleep in Titania's bower. Oberon, on seeing Titania's infatuation, has begun to pity her. He has, however, prevailed upon her to give up to him the boy he had wanted for his page. He drops the juice upon her eyelids and tells Puck to take away the ass-head from Bottom's shoulders. He ordains that all the human characters on waking up, will think that their experiences during the night had only been dreams:

> That he, awaking when the other do,
> May all to Athens back again repair,
> And think no more of this night's account
> But as the fierce vexation of a dream.[3]

By this time it is morning and Theseus, with Hippolyta and the courtiers has come to the forest to hunt. He sees the two pairs of lovers fast asleep on the ground. They are awakened and they recount their adventures in the forest. Now Demetrius is in love with Helena and is no longer willing to marry Hermia, as he was before. Seeing that these four have sorted themselves out in their love-affairs, Theseus overrules Egeus and decides that they too will be married when he himself gets married to Hippolyta on that very day.

These orders are duly carried out and in the last scene everyone assembles in the royal palace and the comic characters present their play. It is a hilarious performance and the mechanicals, in all seriousness, provide wonderful comic entertainment. The courtly characters appreciate and enjoy every moment of it. A dance is presented at the end and as it is midnight all the characters retire.

But the play does not end here, for now the fairies come in. Oberon leads and all the fairies sing and dance. Then Oberon pronounces his blessing on the newly-weds, all the three pairs:

> To the best bride-bed will we,
> Which by us shall blessed be:
> And the issue there create
> Ever shall be fortunate.
> So shall all the couples three
> Ever true in loving be.[4]

Then Puck speaks the Epilogue and the play comes to an end. In the epilogue Puck takes an apologetic tone, asking for the indulgence of the audience. This was quite customary in the plays of the time.

(B) THE GENRE OF THE PLAY

The Dream, which has been designated as the first of his masterpieces, has been generally recognised to be a romantic comedy. There are, however, some differences of opinion as many critics are not satisfied with this term. They feel that the label of romantic comedy is not capable of expressing the nature of the play and have given it other and different names. A few of these terms will now be explained.

(i) Romantic Comedy

The chief characteristic of a romantic comedy is that the main theme of the play is love. Shakespeare wrote many romantic comedies. As a matter of fact, three of the early comedies, *Love's Labour's Lost, The Two Gentlemen of Verona* and the *Dream* are all romantic comedies, as are also the *Golden Comedies* that are to come later. Love is the predominant theme in all of them. In this context, H.B. Charlton has pointed out that, first of all it is this feature that differentiates it from classical plays:

> It is its specific pre-occupation with wooing which distinguishes it most markedly from classical or Roman comedies.[5]

The element of love has certain distinctive features in romantic comedies. In classical comedies the theme is treated far more lightly and love-intrigues are more related to the plot than either to the theme or the characters. This is not so in romantic comedies. Here a maiden has to be courted with great seriousness and has to be won and cherished. Her love is a treasure to be attained with much difficulty. Love itself has become an intense emotion, almost transforming the lover, turning him into a better and nobler person.

It automatically follows that this change in the attitude towards women and to love brought about a drastic change in romantic comedy itself. The evolutionary idea of courtly love and chivalry changed the very nature of romantic comedy:

> Dante had transmuted womankind for men. He had opened their eyes to the image of woman whose coming is as from heaven to reveal a miracle.[6]

It is this attitude of courtly love that is found in Elizabethan romantic comedy. Turning his attention to the *Dream* H.B. Charlton remarks:

> ... and what is a fantasia like *A Midsummer Night's Dream* but the very ecstasy of romance? So the epithet goes unquestioned.[7]

The main theme in a romantic comedy is love and therefore the main characters in such a play are lovers, and the plot is concerned with the ultimate end of love—marriage. The intrigues in such a plot also arise out of the theme of love. In the *Dream* the right note is struck in the very beginning when Theseus announces that he and Hippolyta are going to get married in four days. After this, with the entrance of the main characters the nature of the play becomes strongly emphasized for here are three young pairs in love with each other and later the group of characters expand into four as Helena is also included. The lovers, however, are at cross-purposes and things become more and more complex in the forest for the magic juice brings about bewildering changes in their allegiances. Lysander and Demetrius both fall in love with Helena and Hermia is forsaken. Then the fairies intervene again and all tangles are unravelled so that three marriages can be celebrated at the end.

This is the case with the main plot and the human characters. In the fairy world also certain changes are brought about by the administering of the juice but these changes are not as serious as the ones with the humans. Actually there is but one change; Titania falls in love with Bottom who has been mischievously given an ass's head by Puck. This too is changed at the end so that Titania is brought back to her senses and the relationship between her and Oberon becomes harmonious. This in turn has positive repercussions on humans, for they bless the weddings at the end.

The mechanicals or the rustics, too, are not deprived of love. They have their share of it when Bottom is loved by Titania. Again, at the end, they echo the main theme by presenting a play centred around tragic love.

The nature of love presented here varies with the different characters. This aspect shall be dealt with in greater detail in the relevant chapter (*vide* Ch. 6, *Major Themes*, Sec. (a), *infra*). What is more important here is the fact that H.B. Charlton has pointed out that in this play the dramatist takes up the theme of love in such a manner as to elevate the play above mere slapstick comedy to serious comedy. The play shows the serious love of Theseus and Hippolyta in the beginning. It is a love that faces the responsibilities of married life and also the peculiar responsibilities of a royal married couple who not only have to set an example to their subjects but have to provide the kingdom with a responsible future king. Theseus had many love-affairs earlier, but now he takes up the duties of the kingdom:

> Hippolyta, I wooed thee with my sword,
> And won thy love,doing thee injuries;
> But I will wed thee in another key
> With pomp, with triumph and with revelling.[8]

It will be a wedding in which an entire kingdom will take

part. Private pleasure and public pleasure will become one in this wedding.

It is against this background that the love-intrigues of the younger people take place. They too are married at the end of the play. These marriages are in sharp contrast with the happy-go-lucky fairy love in which the lack of domestic responsibilities brings about levity that is all right for fairies but unsuitable for humans. The *Dream* becomes a serious romantic comedy because, says Charlton, it:

> ... looks to the preservation of the whole human race as human beings rather than to the maintenance of a particular social caste.[9]

(ii) City Comedy

Elizabethan comedy has been divided into three distinct categories by M.C. Bradbrook who, like H.B. Charlton, is one of the pioneering authors of moderns times on Elizabethan comedy. She designates this play as a city comedy. First of all, she describes the city comedy. Mainly satirical in tone, these plays are aimed at the audience of young men of the nobility or the gentry. This was in the beginning of the seventeenth century. Then this kind of play underwent a gradual change. The critical strain mixed with the older tradition of plots based on legends, folklore, etc., and this mixture is seen at its best in Shakespeare:

> ... the poet of *A Midsummer Night's Dream* and *Romeo and Juliet*, plays of lyrical beauty and low comedy, wherein it is no longer possible to distinguish separate strands of the older kind of play, for Shakespeare is here creating his own.[10]

Later in her book she couples the *Dream* and Ben Jonson's *Tale of a Tub* as city comedies. By this time Elizabethan comedy had changed. The writers were experimenting, and whichever of the new forms succeeded on the stage came to be copied immediately. There were the 'nocturnals' in which characters were involved in many mistakes made during one night. This was an old form and the new writers of the last decade of the sixteenth century added to it the adventures of runaway lovers.

Magic and fairies were also added to this kind of play and the *Dream* contains all of these elements.

It is still a city comedy as that is the underlying genre of the play. The satire involving the rustics is so gentle that it can hardly be called satire. Shakespeare merely pokes fun at them and produces good-natured laughter. The eloping pair of lovers get involved in the mistakes made by the fairies, falling in and out of love with great rapidity. All these mistakes take place during just one night. Shakespeare has here brought together the old tradition of comedy and the new experiments in so masterly a manner that Bradbrook calls it "the Shakespearean Synthesis:"

> What Shakespeare had achieved in *M.N.D.*
> ... could not be attempted by lesser men.[11]

No better expression of this synthesis can be found than the one given by the poet himself:

> And as imagination bodies forth
> The forms of things unknown, the poet's pen
> Turns them to shapes and gives to airy nothing
> A local habitation and a name.[12]

Though Bradbrook points out that Shakespeare brought about a synthesis of the old and the new, she does not say that the *Dream* is in a new genre but declares it to be a city comedy, with many new elements in it.

(iii) Situation Comedy

This is a well-known concept and the view that the *Dream* is a situation comedy has been held by many writers. The Shakespearean critic who has made a systematic study from this point of view is L.S. Champion. Not only the early plays of Shakespeare, but those of his contemporaries also are situation comedies in which characters are of less importance than plot. The plot or the action presents different comic situations and the characters are manipulated according to these situations:

> There is no significant development of the main characters; instead, they are manipulated into situations which are

humorous as a result, for example, of mistaken identities or slapstick confusions.[13]

The *Dream* is Shakespeare's "final situation comedy." The characteristics as presented by Champion are all present in it. The lovers are plunged into situation after situation to which they have to adjust themselves. Thus in the very beginning Egeus and Theseus together make it impossible for Lysander and Hermia to marry, thus forcing them to elope. At least here the decision for their future course of action is left to them, though actually there is no choice. Hermia has to choose between Demetrius or death or perpetual virginity as the priestess of Diana. This is actually no choice, and she chooses the last:

> So will I grow, so live, so die, my lord,
> Ere I will lead my virgin patent up
> Unto his lordship, whose unwished yoke
> My soul consents not to give sovereignty.[14]

Thus the decision to elope is virtually forced upon them. Then when they reach the forest, the fairies take a hand in their fortunes and they fall in and out of love in a laughter-provoking manner. The situations are such that they have no choice. Lysander's solemn vows to Hermia are swept away when he wakes up after his eyes have been doctored and sees Helena first.

Then the situations become even more complex for the juice is dropped upon Demetrius's eyelids and he consequently falls in love with Helena. Both of these situations are brought about by the fairies and provoke comic laughter. The same is the case with Titania and Bottom, both of whom are like puppets in the hands of Oberon and Puck. As a matter of fact the three human lovers Titania and Bottom are entirely beyond their control—situations which have been predetermined by circumstances (as the Athenian rule) or by outside agents, like Oberon and Puck.

Then, just as arbitrarily as the situation had been made complex, it is put straight again. Lysander comes back to Hermia, Demetrius comes back to fall in love with Helena, Titania is released from her infatuation and Bottom is brought back to his natural state. The comic effects, thus, depend entirely on the situations and not on the characters:

> Determined by the preconceived situation, not as in later plays giving rise to the action as a result of their personalities, these characters are maneuvered from above rather than motivated from within.[15]

Such comedies are also known as narrative comedies, for in them the story is of more importance than the characters. It is in the mature plays of Shakespeare that the characters outstrip the action in importance and influence the entire play. This is the last of such situation comedies by our dramatist.

In addition to these views the *Dream* has also been called "a parody of love" (W. Oechelhäuser), "a masque" (Frank Sidgwick), "a psychological study" (G.K. Chesterton), "a romantic fairy-tale" (W.H. Auden), "a lyric divertissement" (G.K. Hunter), "a psychomachia" (Noel Purdon). The fact that there are so many different views about the genre makes us realize the complexity of the play. While studying such interpretations it should also be kept in mind that the mid-nineteenth century critic J.O. Halliwell-Phillipps had cautioned the over-enthusiastic critic:

> The *Midsummer Night's Dream* is too exquisite a composition to be dulled by the infliction of philosophical analysis.[16]

REFERENCES

1. Watts, C., ed., *A Midsummer Night's Dream*, Act I, Scene i, lines 1-4, p. 33, *Wordsworth Classics*, Ware, 1992. All future references to this text will be to this edition.
2. Act III, Sc. ii, ll 345-46, p. 70.
3. Act IV, sc. i, ll 65-68, p. 75.
4. Act V, sc. i, ll 387-92, p. 93.
5. Charlton, H.B., *Shakespearean Comedy*, London, Methuen & Co. Ltd., University pbk., no date, p. 21.
6. *Ibid.*, p. 21.
7. *Ibid.*, p. 19.
8. Act I, sc. i, lines 16-19, p. 33.
9. Charlton *op. cit.*, p. 120.

10. Bradbrook, M.C., *Growth and Structure of Elizabethan Comedy*, London, Chatto & Windus, 1955, p. 75.
11. *Ibid*., p. 107.
12. Act V, sc. i, ll 14-17, p. 82.
13. Champion, L.S., *The Evolution of Shakespeare's Comedy: A Study in Dramatic Perspective*. Harvard, University Press, 1970, p. 9.
14. Act I, sc. i, ll 79-82, p. 35.
15. Champion, *op. cit*., pp. 49-50.
16. Price, A., ed., Shakespeare: *A Midsummer Night's Dream*: *A Casebook*, London, Palgrave (Macmillan), 1993, p. 40.

5

A Scene-wise Analysis

Act I, Scene i

The play is opened by Theseus and Hippolyta and the chief note of love and marriage which dominates the play is sounded by them right at the outset. Their marriage will take place in four days and Theseus is impatient for these days to be over.

While they are talking Egeus enters with Hermia his daughter, Lysander and Demetrius. The two latter are Hermia's suitors. Egeus favours Demetrius to such an extent that he would marry Hermia to him by force. An ancient rule decrees that a father can sentence his daughter to death if she disobeys him:

> I beg the ancient privilege of Athens:
> As she is mine, I may dispose of her:
> Which should be either to this gentleman,
> Or to her death, according to our law.[1]

Theseus gives her another alternative: she will either die or dedicate herself as a priestess to Diana, and it is the latter that she chooses. Theseus gives her a few days to consider her decision.

She and Lysander decide to run away and marry. At a distance of seven leagues from Athens Lysander's loving aunt lives and this is where they will go for the Athenian law is powerless there. They decide to run away the following night and meet in a forest near Athens. Hermia agrees joyfully to this idea of Lysander who reveals himself as a determined and resourceful person.

Then comes Hermia who is deeply in love with Demetrius. At once a triangular scheme of the plot becomes clear and foundations are laid for future complications. The two lovers confide their plan to Helena, never dreaming that she will betray them at the first opportunity, showing herself to be entirely without honour.

Actually Helena is so deeply in love with Demetrius that she tells him the lovers' plan as she thinks it will please Demetrius and also give her a chance to meet him. What is more, in the blind intensity of her love she does not take two factors into account: (a) in telling Demetrius she will be betraying her friend and, (b) as Hermia is her rival in love, the sooner she gets married the better will it be for her. In enabling Demetrius to follow the eloping lovers she is defeating her own ends. It is surprising that she does not think of this very practical issue.

Thus, in this very first scene the action has already started to take shape. It will be noticed that there is no prologue to this play. In Elizabethan plays the prologue is often included within the first scene and that is the case here. The first nineteen lines are like a prologue and then with the entrance of Egeus and the others the action starts. The scene can actually be divided into three sections thus:

(i) Lines 1-19: the dialogue between Theseus and Hipployta which serves as a prologue, introducing the theme.

(ii) Lines 20-137: Egeus *et al.,* enter and ultimatum is given to Hermia. All except the lovers go out.

(iii) Lines 138 till the end: the lovers plan their elopement and confide in Helena.

Thus the scene looks forward to the second part of the first scene of Act II in which Demetrius and Helena enter the forest. It is also linked with the second part of the second scene of Act II for there the two lovers enter the forest. Throughout the play there is this kind of interlinking.

The scene is rich in many notable features of rhetoric and versification. These will be analysed in a later and relevant chapter (*vide* Ch. 10 and 11, *infra*). It is entirely in verse, as there are only noble characters in it. This is typical of Elizabethan plays.

Act I, sc. ii

The comic characters are now introduced. There are six of them, all belonging to the working class and have been called "the mechanicals" or "the rustics". There is Peter Quince who is a carpenter and whose surname refers to a wooden wedge used in carpentry. Thus his name shows his trade and this is the case with all six of them (*vide* Ch. 8, *Minor Characters*, *infra*). There is Bottom, the weaver who is the most memorable character of this play, Flute, Snout, Snug and Starveling. All of them have gathered together for, like loyal subjects, they want to celebrate the royal wedding by entertaining him and his bride with a play.

The play they decide to perform is one about Pyramus and Thisby. This is a story of tragic love, and so, unsuitable for a wedding. The rustics however are too ignorant to know this. They do not even know the difference between tragedy and comedy.

Quince: Marry, our play is "The Most Lamentable comedy and Most Cruel Death of Pyramus and Thisby."

Bottom: A very good piece of work, I assure you, and a merry.[2]

The different roles are allotted by Quince. He gives the role of Pyramus to Bottom who is sure he will shine in it. Now Flute, whose name makes one think that perhaps he has got a soft fluting voice, is given the role of Thisby. Starveling is given the role of Thisby's mother and Snout that of the father of Pyramus. Quince himself will take on the role of Thisby's father and Snug will play the Lion. Here some trouble arises for Bottom would dearly like to play the Lion. Quince manages to dissuade him. The dialogues are distributed and they decide to meet in the forest the next night, as they want to rehearse in privacy. Quince is the director-cum-manager-cum-producer, and all assure him that they will learn their dialogues and be present in the forest on time. Then they disperse.

This is one of the shortest scenes in the play, containing a total of ninety-eight lines. It is entirely in prose and it must be remembered that in prose the number of lines vary with different editions, unlike in poetry. The scene is in prose as all the characters in it are humble ones. Usually in Elizabethan plays, poetry is kept for the noble characters and prose for the humble ones, though there are exceptions. The scene has a song also, the first song in the play, sung by Bottom (*vide* Ch. 11, Poetic Style, *infra.*).

The scene is important because the comic sub-plot is introduced in it. As yet it has no interlinking with the main plot. That is, it does not look back to the first scene. It does, however, look forward to the first scene of Act III. Thus Shakespeare weaves the different strands of the play together. The entire scene is written with great good humour. He has parodied the actors and managers of his day, but there is no satire involved here. There is only good-natured fun. This kind of humour, which has no malice or satire in it, is very rare to find. He is one of the very few writers who can give it to us.

Again, the scene highlights one of the important features of Elizabethan plays—the lack of actresses so that the female role had to be played by young men. Flute is made to take up the role of Thisby, although he has "a beard coming." Dr. Johnson remarks:

> It is observed in Downe's *Memoirs of the Playhouses* that one of these counterfeit heroines moved the passions more strongly than the women that have since been brought upon the stage.[3]

The first Act comes to an end with this scene. All the Act in this play are short and contain only two scenes The play itself, as a matter of fact, is one of the shortest of Shakespeare's plays. The first Act usually introduces all the main characters and begins the action. In this play, however, all the main characters have not been introduced as yet, for the fairies are still to come. The action, however, has started already, for the chief characters of the main plot and all the comic characters have already decided, though independently, to meet in the forest. This Act is located in Athens, the first scene in the Duke's palace and the second in Quince's house. After this there will be a total change of scenery, for which Shakespeare has already prepared us. The last scene of the play, like the first, shall be located in the Duke's palace so that, place-wise, the plot completes a circular motion.

Act II, Sc. i

The supernatural characters are now going to be introduced. The scene opens with Puck (or Robin Goodfellow) talking to a fairy. It becomes clear through their conversation that the King and the Queen of the fairies have quarrelled violently with each other over a little human boy. The mother of their boy was a friend and priestess of Titania and she died after bringing the child into the world. Titania then looked after the boy who was a very captivating child, and kept him as her page. Now Oberon also wants the same boy for one of his knights but Titania will not give him up. This has created so much conflict between the two of them that they quarrel whenever they meet.

While Puck and the fairy are talking about this, the King and the Queen enter. They start quarrelling as soon as they meet, accusing each other of unfaithfulness. Titania describes how their quarrelling has brought about great disturbance in the world of nature but when Oberon points out that she can bring back peace and harmony by giving him the boy, she refuses outright.

> But she, being mortal, of that boy did die;
> And for her sake do I rear up the boy;
> And for her sake I will not part with him.[4]

Then Titania goes away and Oberon unfolds his plan to Puck. Here follows one of the loveliest passages of the play. Oberon was once listening to the song of a mermaid when he saw, up in the sky, Cupid shooting his arrow of love at a certain divine priestess. This arrow, however missed its mark:

> ... young Cupid's fiery shaft
> Quenched in the chaste beams of the wat'ry moon.
> And the imperial vot'ress passed on
> In maiden meditation, fancy-free.[5]

This arrow, missing its mark, fell on a flower which turned purple though it was white before. The juice of this flower, put on the eyelids of a sleeping person will make him or her fall in love with the first person he or she sees on waking up. He tells Puck to bring this herb so that he may drop the juice on Titania's eyes when she is asleep. Then she will fall in love with whichever creature she sees on waking up and then he will get the boy from her as the price of undoing the charm he had put on her.

While he is waiting for Puck, Demetrius and Helena enter. Demetrius is annoyed with Helena for having followed him. Seeing the suffering of Helena's one-sided love, Oberon who had been observing them while he himself is invisible, decides to put the love-juice on Demetrius and make him love her. When Puck returns he gives a little of the juice to him, telling him to put the juice on Demetrius's eyes. He cautions Puck that this must be done in such a way that Demetrius must see Helena first on waking up:

> A sweet Athenian lady is in love
> With a disdainful youth: anoint his eyes—
> But do it when the next thing he espies
> May be the lady.[6]

The Athenians, however, have left the stage by this time, so Puck has not seen them. This is the root of all trouble, for later he will see the eloping lovers and mistake them for the former pair. This scene comes to an end here.

In this scene the third group of characters, the fairies, have been introduced, so that all the characters are now known to the audience.

The scene is divisible into three parts. The first part ends with line no. 197 when Demetrius and Helena enter the stage. The second part, starting with their entrance, continues till line no. 244 when they leave. The third part, starting with Oberon's directions to Puck, promises future complications, for the audience knows that Demetrius and Helena are not the only human beings in the forest, for Lysander and Hermia are also there. A slight mistake on Puck's part will lead to great confusion. The ensuing events fulfill the hopes and fears of the audience in full measure.

The second part of the scene looks, back to the first scene of the play and forward to the next one. The first and the third parts of the scene do not have any preceding links but they drastically influence the action in the ensuing scene.

The entire scene, as it deals with supernatural entities and noble characters, is in verse. Shakespeare uses blank verse as well as couplets here. A large section of the first part is in couplets. There is also one of the loveliest songs in Shakespeare, sung by the fairy whom Puck meets. This is the second song of the play.

Shakespeare has now introduced all the characters of the play and the action has started to take shape, for the audience has started to anticipate future events. But there are still surprises. Moreover, in this scene Demetrius and Helena have reached the forest but the other pair and all the six mechanicals are still to reach it. Complications in the plot are only being anticipated in this scene, they have not yet taken place.

Act II, sc. ii

Here we see Titania with her retinue. She assigns different tasks to different fairies and then prepares for sleep. The fairies sing a lovely lullaby to put her to sleep—the third song of the play. Then when she is asleep the fairies go away and Oberon enters. He drips the juice upon her eyelids, chanting a few lines at the same time which enjoins upon her to love the creature she sees on waking up. He even tells her, to wake up when some ugly creature is near:

> When thou wak'st it is thy dear,
> Wake when some vile creature is near.[7]

After he has gone Lysander and Hermia enter. They are being seen in the forest for the first time. Hermia is tired with walking in the forest, for Lysander has lost the way, so they decide to lie down and rest for a while.

While they are sleeping, Puck enters. He has been searching the forest for a pair of Athenians. Finding Lysander and

Hermia, he takes them for the ones Oberon had meant. He drips the juice upon Lysander's eyes and leaves. Immediately after this Demetrius and Helena arrive. By this time Demetrius is very angry with Helena for following him about and leaving her he walks off.

Helena stands alone in the dark and laments her fate. Seeing Lysander asleep she wakes him and as soon as he opens his eyes he falls violently in love with her. This is the first example of the power of the love-juice. Helena, faced with this sudden change, treats it as a cruel joke and leaves the place. Lysander follows her. Then Hermia wakes up and finding herself alone, goes out in search of him. The scene ends here.

This scene, though not very long (containing 164 lines) is yet the most eventful scene so far. Part of it is concerned with the fairies and part with the humans. Thus, it falls into two clear-cut sections, the first section ending with the departure of Oberon after putting the juice on Titania's eyelids and the second section lasting from here till the end. The scene is linked with the former scene in which the plan of Oberon had been explained and it naturally looks forward to the second scene of the next Act in which we meet the characters again.

The scene shows great variety in versification as it contains three kinds of verse dialogues and a song. Blank verse is used in the beginning when Titania speaks to her attendants. Then there is a song, the third in the play. After this Oberon chants in trochaic tetrametre couplets. Then the Athenians speak in heroic couplets. Puck speaks in octosyllabic couplets just like Oberon. Thus not only does the scene take the action forward but presents great variety in versification as well.

This is the last scene of this Act and takes us to the middle of the play. As yet the comic characters have not reached the forest but the two serious plots have already been brought together, as Oberon takes a hand in the lovers' affairs. Complications have already started with Lysander falling in love with Hermia. The next Act will prove more complex.

Act III, Sc. i

This scene shows us the comic characters who have now

reached the forest. Titania is asleep in the background and none of them can see her. They proceed with the business of rehearsing the play. Bottom points out that Pyramus's suicide may not be popular with the soft-hearted ladies in the audience and so he suggests that a prologue should be written to explain to the audience that actually he is not Pyramus but Bottom the weaver and that he is not really killing himself. The same will be done for Snug who will be playing the lion which again, might frighten the ladies. When these points are settled they realise that they have to provide for the moon, so it is decided that someone will have to bring a lantern to stand for the moon. Moreover, a wall has to be provided also, for Pyramus and Thisby used to talk through a chink in the wall that separated their houses. So they decide that someone will stand with arms outspread to show the wall. Shakespeare shows what shifts the poor dramatic groups were put to when performing.

While they are discussing all this. Puck enters and is highly amused and entertained and decides to watch them. By this time the actual rehearsal has started. Bottom, who is Pyramus leaves the stage for a few minutes. Puck takes this opportunity to put an ass's head on him. When he enters on cue, everyone is amazed and frightened. They exclaim and run off. He, of course, does not realise that he has been transformed. Left alone he thinks that the others have planned to frighten him. He decides that he will walk about and sing to show that he is not afraid of being alone.

He starts to sing and has sung but one stanza when Titania, who had been asleep all this time, wakes up. She promptly falls in love with him, giving us the second example of the power of the love-juice:

> I pray thee, gentle mortal, sing again
> Mine ear is much enamoured of thy note
> So is mine eye enthralled to thy Shape.[8]

She tells him that she loves him. Bottom is a man of sound common sense and reacts accordingly, telling her that it is most unrealistic, but then love and realism do not go together. Titania calls all her attendants and tells them to serve Bottom.

Bottom is introduced to each of the four fairies. He talks to each of them very courteously. Then he is led away to Titania's bower and the scene ends.

This scene, from the point of view of the overall structure of the play, occupies a crucial position. In all, there are nine scenes in the play and this is the fifth. That is to say, it is the central scene of the play. In it the dramatist weaves the three strands of the play together, bringing all the characters of the play on the stage. The Athenians are influenced by the fairies, and they, willy-nilly, become concerned with the rustics. It, thus, looks back at the former scenes and forward to the next.

It can be neatly divided into two parts. The first part ends just before Titania awakens and the second part starts with her awakening and falling in love with Bottom. This division is flexible, for the dividing line can be drawn earlier, when Bottom enters with the ass-head.

The first part is written in prose, except for the dialogue of Pyramus and Thisby. It is a highly humorous depiction of a theatrical rehearsal by a group of ignorant rustics. One of the earliest opinions is that of Dr. Johnson:

> In the time of Shakespeare there were many companies of players.... Of these some were undoubtedly very unskilful and very poor and it is probable that the design of this scene is to ridicule their ignorance and the odd expedients to which they might be driven by want of proper decorations.[9]

The design might be to ridicule, but there is no malice in the way in which Shakespeare pokes fun at these characters. These are comic and not satirical characters. The dramatist wants to provide good-natured laughter, he is not criticizing.

The scene contains both prose and verse, for the rustics converse in prose and the fairies in verse. There is some variety in versification as well. Puck uses quatrains as well as heroic couplets and blank verse. It also contains a song sung by Bottom, which is the fourth song in the play.

There is an interesting observation by Dr. Johnson regarding one of the nature images in this scene Titania says:

> And light them at the fiery glow-worm's eyes.[10]

This offends Dr. Johnson's strong common sense and he remarks:

> I know not how Shakespeare who commonly derived his knowledge of nature from his own observations, happened to place the flow-worms' light in his eyes, which is only in his tail.[11]

Act III, Sc. ii

The scene opens with Oberon wondering if Titania is awake and whom she has fallen in love with. Puck arrives and tells him about the six comic characters whom he calls "a crew of patches, rude mechanicals." He tells Oberon of how he has fixed an ass-head on Bottom and how Titania is now in love with him. Then Oberon asks him if he has put the love-juice on the Athenian's eyes and Puck has hardly finished assuming him that he has done so when Demetrius and Hermia enter. Demetrius is still pleading his suit and Hermia very much suspects that he has harmed Lysander in some way. She goes away in search of him and Demetrius, by now grown tired, lies down to rest.

By this time both Oberon and Puck have realised that Puck had put the love-juice on the eyelids of the wrong person. So Oberon rebukes Puck and tells him to go and bring Helena to this place by some means or other. When he goes, Oberon drips the juice upon Demetrius's eyelids. Within a few minutes Puck returns followed by Helena and Lysander. Lysander is still in love with her and overwhelms her with protestation of his sincerity. As they are talking, Demetrius wakes and falls in love with Helena at once.

Helena cannot believe that he is serious and thinks him to be mocking her. Now the position has become truly ridiculous as both the men none of whom had loved her, are now deeply enamoured of her. A little later Hermia enters. Her position now is that of Helena's as it formerly was. None of the men desires her, though she loves Lysander. A violent quarrel breaks out and the two men get ready for a fight. They go out together and then the two girls also, totally bewildered, leave the stage. The love-intrigues thus reach the highest peak of complexity.

Oberon and Puck had been overlooking the entire affair. Oberon thinks that Puck, being a mischievous spirit has deliberately brought about this complication and Puck protests his innocence. Oberon then directs him to create a dark mist in order to separate the two men. Then he will have to lead them astray, making them wander all over the forest so that they will get tired and lie down to sleep. Then he will put the juice of another flower on Lysander's eyelids which will bring back his love for Hermia. He ordains that whatever had happened during the night will seem to be like a dream to all of them as they wake up.

> When they next wake, all this derision
> Shall seem a dream and fruitless vision.[12]

Meanwhile he himself will disenchant Titania and get the little boy from her.

Puck then sets about his duties. Demetrius comes and Puck, assuming the voice of Lysander, leads him away. Then Lysander comes, very tired, and lies down to sleep. After a while Demetrius also comes and lies down. Then one by one the two girls come and each lies down near her beloved. Puck then, singing the sixth song of the play, drips the juice upon Lysander's eyelids. The scene ends here.

This is the longest scene of the play, comprising 464 lines. It can be divided into five sections. The first section, till line 40, contains the dialogue between Oberon and Puck. Then the second section begins with the entrance of Demetrius and Hermia. Then, with Hermia's exit and Demetrius's lying down to rest in line 87, this section ends. The dialogue between Oberon and Puck makes up the third section. Then Helena and Lysander enter in line 122 and section 4 starts. This fourth section is the longest, from line 122 to 344. In the last section everything is sorted out and Puck sings the well-known song that has gained the status of a proverb:

> Jack shall have Jill;
> Naught shall go ill;

The man shall have his mare again
And all shall be well.[13]

The scene is integrally linked to the former and the ensuing scenes. The love-complications among the humans had been brought about in the former scene and here they are on the way to being resolved. But as the problems will be solved in the next scene so this scene anticipates the later ones. Again, the fairy-plot and the rustic-plot had been brought together in the former scene when Titania was made to fall in love with Bottom. Now Oberon, on being told about Titania's condition, decides that he will disenchant her. So, though Titania and Bottom are not on the stage in this scene, their fate has been decided and the scene looks forward to the next. Thus all the scenes are being, like the plots, firmly interlinked.

As far as versification goes, there is great variety in this scene. Blank verse, heroic couplets, octosyllabic couplets and song, all have been used, but the heroic couplet is the most prominent. About three-fourths of the dialogue is in heroic couplets. There are 106 heroic couplets, i.e. 212 lines. The Athenians speak in heroic couplets as well as in triplets and quatrains. A song, the sixth in the play, is sung by Puck.

Though it is such a long scene, full of confusing events. Yet Shakespeare has written it so skillfully that the hand of a master is everywhere seen quite evidently.

Act IV, Sc. i

The scene is opened by Titania, her attendant fairies and Bottom. Titania is deeply enamoured of Bottom and is trying to please him in all the ways she can. Oberon himself invisible, watches the whole scene. The four attendant Moth, Peae-blossom, Cobweh and Mustardseed are set different tasks by Bottom and then both Titania and Bottom fall asleep, with Titania lovingly encircling Bottom's head with her arms.

When Puck enters, Oberon tells him how a little while ago he had upbraided Titania for her infatuation and she had been apologetic about it. He had then asked her to surrender the little boy over whom they had fallen out and she had done so without further argument. This was all that he had wanted. So, now that his purpose has been served, he decides to set her free of the spell. So he drips the antidote upon her eyelids and as she wakes up, she sees him in front of her and greets him lovingly. Oberon then orders Puck to take away Bottom's ass-head and this is done at once, though Bottom does not know it, for he is still sleeping. The fairies play music and Oberon tells Titania that they will dance at Theseus's wedding which is to take place on the morrow, blessing their union.

Dawn is breaking and they must retire now. Oberon says they will follow the night around the globe:

Trip we after the night's shade
We the globe can compass soon
Swifter than the wandering moon.[14]

Now another day has dawned and Theseus, with Hippolyta, Egeus and others, has come to the forest to hunt. At first Theseus and Hippolyta talk about hunting then suddenly his attention is caught by the sleeping figure of Hermia, and Egeus spots the others. They are awakened and Theseus asks for an explanation of their presence. Lysander answers him but all of them are so confused that they do not know what had really happened. They do not know whether they had been dreaming or whether they are truly awake now. Theseus roundly declares that he will override Egeus and the two pairs will get married at the same time that he and Hippolyta get married. Then the royal party goes away and the four lovers wonder about their experiences during the night. Demetrius expresses their general feeling of bewilderment:

Are you sure
That we are awake? It seems to me
That yet we dream.[15]

All four of them decide to go to Athens and leave the stage.

The stage, however, is not empty for Bottom is there, sleeping through it all. He wakes only now, when he is alone on the stage. he is sorely puzzled and finally decides that he has had a wonderful dream. This speech is a short one and a famous one:

> I have had a dream—past the wit of man to say what dream it was: man is but an ass, if he go about to expound this dream.[16]

This scene is divisible into two clear sections. The first section ends with the departure of the fairies in line 102 and the next section lasts till the end. The two sections are almost equal in length. Moreover, the two halves are so managed that the first section takes place before daybreak and the second in the morning. This morning, Shakespeare tells us, is the morning of May day, because, referring to the lovers, Theseus says:

> No doubt they rose up early, to observe
> The rite of May.[17]

This means that the night when all these confusions took place was the night before May day, and not Midsummer night. This fact had irritated Dr. Johnson, who liked consistency:

> I know not why Shakespeare calls this play a *Midsummer Night's Dream* when he so carefully informs us that it happened on the night preceding May day![18]

This is a crucial scene as in it all complications are unravelled and the dramatist takes us back to the ordinary world once more. Again, in his characteristic way, the scene combines the elements of all the three plots. The first half is concerned with both the fairy-plot and the mechanicals-plot. That the second plot which brings us back to daylight and the ordinary world, is concerned with the Athenians. The last speech spoken by Bottom links it once more with the mechanicals.

The term 'dream' of the title is used many times in this scene. It is first used by Oberon:

> And think no more of this night's accidents
> But as the fierce vexation of a dream.[19]

Then Demetrius uses it (in the lines quoted earlier) and finally Bottom used it no less than six times in his speech. The dramatist lays emphasis on the fact that all that had happened is to be taken as lightly as a dream—a dream which is strange and wonderful but like a dream it has vanished. The only result, as the audience knows, is the fact that Demetrius, who used to be in love with Hermia and scorn Helena is now devoted to the latter. So all tangles are now straightened out and three marriages can take place.

The scene has great variety in versification. There is blank verse, spoken by Oberon, Titania and the Athenians and prose spoken by Bottom. There are also two songs. One of them is sung or perhaps chanted by Oberon and the other sung by all the three fairies, King, Queen and servant:

> Now thou and I are new in amity,
> And will tomorrow midnight solemnly
> Dance in Duke Theseus' house triumphantly.[20]

Act IV, Sc. ii

Shakespeare takes up the mechanicals in this scene. Once more the scene, like the second scene of Act I, is set in Quince's house. All except Bottom are present. He is such a forceful an important character that without him the play cannot be staged:

> Quince: It is not possible; you have
> not a man in all Athens able
> to discharge Pyramus but he
>
> Flute: No; he hath simply the best
> way of any handicraft man
> in Athens.[21]

While they are lamenting the absence of Bottom the man himself turns up. The others are eager to hear his adventures, but Bottom is a very sensible, practical man. He is not going to boast about himself when there is work to be done. The Duke and the others have got married already and have taken their dinner. Now is the time for their play to be performed. There is no time to sit and gossip. Bottom hustles them all away to prepare for the performance.

This is a very short scene—the shortest in the play. As it deals only with the mechanicals it is entirely in prose. It serves the useful purpose of telling us that the three marriages have already been solemnised and prepares us for the play that is going to be put up by Bottom and his friends. It is actually like a link scene between the preceding and the following one.

It also brings the fourth Act to an end. This has been an Act of unravelling, for in it we have seen Titania being released from the spell that made her love Bottom, Bottom freed from the ass-head, the tangle among the lovers sorted out and Egeus overridden by Theseus, declaring that Lysander is to be married to Hermia. This harmony is restored in the human world. In the fairy world also harmony has been re-established, for the King and the Queen are not quarrelling any longer. Instead they decide to come and bless the triple wedding. Shakespeare, however does not end the play here, for the mechanicals have to stage their play and expectations have been carefully built up on the audience for this performance.

Act V, Sc. i

This is the last scene of the play. The lover have, by this time, told Theseus about their adventures in the forest which they think to be a dream. Theseus is very sceptical. He too thinks that these wonderful experiences cannot be true. He compares lovers with poets and lunatics. This is one of the most famous passages in Shakespeare:

> The lunatic, the lover and the poet
> Are of imagination all compact:
> One sees more devils than vast hell can hold
> That is the madman: The lover, all as frantic
> Sees Helen's beauty in a brow of Egypt
> The poets eye, in a fine frenzy rolling.
> Doth glance from heaven to earth, from earth to heaven.
>
> And as imagination bodies forth
> The forms of things unknown, the poet's pen
> Turns them to shapes, and gives to airy nothing.
> A local habitation and a name.[22]

The four lovers, happily married, enter next and after welcoming them Theseus wants to know what arrangements have been made for entertainments to celebrate the occasion. They have three hours before they retire for rest and everyone wants some entertainment.

Philostrate, the Master of Revels gives him a list of the proposed entertainments to choose from. Theseus's attention is attracted by the extraordinary title of *Pyramus and Thisby*.

> A tedious brief scene of young Pyramus
> And his love Thisby; very tragical mirth.[23]

He decides to have this play for his entertainment. Hippolyta tries to dissuade him, telling him that it is not worthy of him. Theseus responds like a noble king and says that it is not the actual performance that is important, but the spirit in which it is presented. The play might be poor and the actors humble ones, but they are presenting it with great sincerity and loyalty. He had seen people falter and stammer and fail to properly welcome him, but he had taken all that in the spirit in which it had been intended. This is what makes us respect him as a mature noble-spirited person—a good king who loves his subjects.

The play starts and first of all comes the Prologue. His speech is unique. It is written very humbly and respectfully but Shakespeare, by changing the punctuation marks, makes it sound like nonsense and the courtly characters comment upon this feature. Then the other characters, i.e. Pyramus, Thisby, the Wall, the Moon and the Lion all enter. The Prologue introduces them and tells the story of the play. The Wall introduces himself. By this time the courtly characters have started to enjoy the whole thing:

> Theseus: Would you desire lime and hair to speak better?
>
> Demetrius: It is the wittiest partition that ever I heard discourse, my lord.[24]

The play proceeds, in bombastic language and the courtly characters commenting good-humouredly and enjoying the show. They also applaud and encourage the actors. Lion and Moonshine come. The Lion tells the ladies in the audience not to be afraid of him for he is no Lion, but Snug the joiner. Moonshine tells the audience that the lantern in his hand is the moon and he himself is the Man in the moon. Then the action proceeds. The Lion roars and Thisby runs off. Then Pyramus comes in and seeing Thisby's mantle torn by the Lion assumes that she is dead and kills himself. Then Thisby comes and seeing Pyramuśs dead body, also kills herself.

Bottom then comes and asks whether the audience would like an epilogue or a dance. Theseus rejects the epilogue but welcomes the dance. After the dance they decide to retire. Theseus declares that they will continue the festivities for two weeks and then they all retire to rest.

Very often at this point, some editors end this scene and begin another with the entrance of the fairies. Again, often enough, the scene of the fairies is included within this one and the same scene. Editors as well directors are actually at liberty to do so, since, originally, the plays were written as a continuous whole. The Act and scene divisions were introduced by the stage managers.

At first it is Puck who enters and sings a song. He is carrying a broom as, according to tradition, he is thought to be a broom-wielder. After his song Oberon and Titania enter with their retinue and they too sing. Then Oberon leads a dance in which all the fairies join. Oberon then sings (or perhaps chants) another song. After this comes the epilogue delivered by Puck. He asks the audience to excuse any faults of the actors by thinking that all this is but a dream:

> That you have but slumbered here
> While these visions did appear
> And this weak and idle theme
> No more yielding but a dream

The scene and, indeed, the play itself, ends with this epilogue. This one long scene makes up the whole of the fifth Act. This is often the ease with his plays—the last Act comprises only one scene. As has been observed above, some editors split this scene into two, giving scene ii from the time that Puck and the other fairies enter and dance. W.J. Craig has done so in his edition.

This concluding scene thus brings the play to its desired end. It concludes with three marriages and the reconciliation of the fairy King and Queen. Thus, both in the natural and in the supernatural world harmony reigns and the aims of romantic comedy have been attained. There is also the impression of a peaceful and prosperous life in the entire kingdom under a just, able and dutiful king. Theseus is one of the ideal kings of Shakespeare, like King Henry V. As it is the last scene, instead of looking forward to future scenes (which will give an impression of inconclusiveness) it should give us a sense of finality and this is exactly what it does. All the three plots come together in it and the poet imparts a sense of effortless ease in weaving them together. Here the serious and the comic are brought together without any impression of incongruity, for the masque presented excites comic laughter and yet it is entirely in tune with the mood of the scene. Moreover, though in the earlier scenes probability might have been stretched a bit too far, that does not happen here. The rustics' presentation of the play is not only probable it is expected as a part of marriage celebration. The ways in which they improvise the requirements of the play, too do not cause surprise, as they have been discussed and thrashed out in an earlier scene (Act III, sc. i.).

The scene has a mixture of verse and prose. The noble characters speak in verse among themselves but when they talk in between the dialogues of the masque they do so in prose. The masque is mostly in quatrains but at times there are couplets too. There are several songs in the scene. Three of them occur in the masque and three more are sung by the fairies. At the end occurs the epilogue, in trochaic tetrametre couplets. This ensures great metrical variation,which is very necessary in a scene as long as this one is.

REFERENCES

1. Act I, sc. i, ll. 41-44, p. 34.
2. Act I, sc. ii, ll. 10-12, p. 40.
3. Price, A., *op. cit.*, p 29.
4. Act II, sc. i, ll. 135-37, p. 46.
5. Act II, sc. i, ll. 163-64, p. 47.
6. Act II, sc. i, ll. 260-63, p. 50.
7. Act II, sc. ii, ll. 41-2. p. 51.
8. Act III, sc. ii, ll. 125-27, p. 58.

9. Price, A., *op. cit.*, p. 29.
10. Act III, sc. i, ll. 156, p. 59.
11. Price, A., *op. cit.*, p. 29.
12. Act III, sc. ii, ll. 376-78, p. 71.
13. Act III, sc. ii, ll. 461-64, p. 73.
14. Act IV, sc. i, ll. 95-98, p. 76.
15. Act IV, sc. i, ll. 192-94, p. 79.
16. Act IV, sc. i, ll. 203-05, p. 79.
17. Act IV, sc. i, ll. 131-32, p. 77.
18. Price, A., *op. cit.*, p. 29.
19. Act IV, sc. i, ll. 67-68, p. 75.
20. Act IV, sc. i, ll. 86-88, p. 76.
21. Act IV, sc. ii, ll. 5-8, p. 80.
22. Act IV, sc. i, ll. 7-17, p. 82.
23. Act IV, sc. i, ll. 56-57, p. 84.
24. Act IV, sc. i, ll. 164-66, p. 86.

6

The Major Themes

It is not enough for a play to have a tight plot-structure for it to gain unity. The plot might observe all the three rules of unity (*vide* Ch. 9, *infra*) and yet the play itself might give an impression of fragmentariness if it does not have a unifying theme. The playwright, in other words, is bound to have a certain idea to convey to the reader or the audience. This might be a philosophical message, a moral lesson, an aesthetic concept, etc. Sometimes the writer may have a theme in his mind and sometimes he may start with the vague idea of telling a story and then gradually a central theme will emerge as he writes. This latter is what most frequently happens in novels and plays. It might also be, as is the case with Shakespeare, that the author's intentions are not known to the reader and the reader finds the unifying theme only after close study. In such cases it is possible, indeed, inevitable, that there might be many interpretations of the same work by different readers and this is what has happened with Shakespeare. His mature plays have given rise to many interpretations and even the *Dream,* early work though it is, has given us quite a few interpretations. This variety does not mean that the work is vague and aimless. Quite the opposite, for multiplicity of meanings implies that the work itself is a complex one. Moreover, there is another factor that adds to this complexity. In addition to there being one central theme or more, there might also be certain ideas that are important and so recur again and again. As Fluchere has pointed out:

> There are minor themes, ceremonial themes, major themes symbolic themes; sometimes set out *en clair*, sometimes developed at length and sometimes, on the contrary, just suggested.[1]

Keeping all these factors in mind, we shall now cast a glance at the variety of themes that literary critics have found in the *Dream*.

(A) THE THEME OF LOVE

(i) It has already been pointed out (*vide* Ch. 2, sec. (b) Genre, sub-section (i) Romantic Comedy, *supra*) that the *Dream* is a romantic comedy and, as is the case with all such plays, the central theme is love. This is the generally accepted view, but within this central theme there are many interpretations about Shakespeare's treatment of this theme.

H.B. Charlton takes a very serious view. According to him Shakespeare accepts the importance and influence of love on men and is trying to determine the social perspective of love:

> "What is the place of love in life?" is the question underlying *A Midsummer Night's Dream*.[2]

In the play we find romantic love in all its intensity. Thus Lysander courts Hermia in the approved Petrarchan manner, serenading her and also sending her love-tokens. For them it is all for love and the world well lost, as Hermia proves when she says that she would rather remain a virgin priestess all her life than marry a man she does not love. They use the language and imagery of courtly love when speaking to each other:

Lysander: How now, my love? Why is your cheek so pale?
How chance the roses there do fade so fast?
Hermia: Belike for want of rain, which I could well
Beteem them from the tempest of my eyes.[3]

Yet, Charlton points out that though they are so wrapped up in each other, the lovers are not in any way isolated from the real world. Their love is not "a prescribed attitude." Jealousy and quarrels make this love the love of the real world and not an idle one. When the mistakes of the night are over the pairs of lovers will take their rightful place in society as responsible citizens, not as idle dreamers.

This is to be parallelled and contrasted with the entirely undomestic and irresponsible love between Oberon and Titania. They are fairies and so their love is very different from human love. It is a love that depends on whims and fancies and can be easily upset by wrangling of possessive spirits over a little boy. One cannot judge them by human standards for, as Charlton points out, if they had human standards they would not have been fairies. Yet, it is this fact itself which sets their kind of love apart from human love. Thus Charlton says:

> The more fairy, the less fitting for the responsibilities of the settled human institution of marriage.[4]

Finally we have the love of the royal couple, Theseus and Hippolyta. There is a mature love here, as intense as responsible. Theseus is aware of the fact that he had not been the ideal lover to Hippolyta:

> Hippolyta, I wooed thee with my sword
> And won thy love, doing thee injuries.[5]

The consciousness of this shortcoming makes him all the more determined to marry her in the proper royal and religious manner. It has to be remembered that. Theseus had many love-affairs in the past, four of which are mentioned by Oberon, but in this play he is the very embodiment of a cool-headed, balanced and just king. He will marry and provide the kingdom with an heir as well as hold up an example of domestic love and security.

All the three plots, thus, converge to the same point—the establishment of a love that is solidly founded on social responsibilities, ensuring the continuity of the human race. The love of the fairies is there to provide a contrast. Yet they come to bless the union of the humans:

> To the best bride-bed will we
> Which by us shall blessed be
> And the issue there create

> Ever shall be fortunate
> ....
> Through this palace, with sweat peace
> And the owner of it blest
> Ever shall in safety rest.[6]

It is this seriousness in the treatment of the theme of love that, for Charlton, makes the play a serious comedy:

> The comedy in *A Midsummer Night's Dream* looks to the preservation of the whole human race as human beings rather than to the maintenance of a particular social caste.[7]

It may be observed in passing that though Charlton speaks of the life led by the fairies as undomestic and irresponsible this is not the view held by all the literary critics (*vide* Ch. 8, *infra*).

(ii) A very different view of the theme of love is taken by other literary critics. Love is looked upon as a kind of madness—an intense emotion that temporarily bereaves man of reason and good sense. But here also there are two kinds of love, the "doting love" which, though intense, is brought about by the eyes and has little that is enduring about it, and true love—a product of the mind, intense and enduring. This classification of love depends upon the contemporary philosophical attitude to love—the rational love and the irrational. These two types were generally accepted, as becomes clear when Bottom says:

> ... and yet, to say the truth, reason and love keep little company together.[8]

This doting love, or love fancy, leads ultimately to tragedy—a tragedy which is exemplified in the playlet put up by the mechanicals. It is blind love and often goes unrequited. It has been pointed out that this doting, blind love, as presented in the play, is of two kinds:

> "Dotage" in this play appears essentially reserved for two kinds of amorous excesses approaching madness: the monomaniacal pursuit of unrequited love (thus Helena "dotes" in idolatry, Demetrius "dotes" on Helena)... or

> the ridiculous bestowal of affection upon an obviously unworthy object (most grotesquely in Titania's passion for Bottom).[9]

This mad, blind, doting love is contrasted with the sane love of Theseus and Hippolyta. Contemporary religious and social concepts of marriage provide a solid background here. This love is a divine force that holds the world and the elements together. Chaucer in *The Knight's Tale* gives an account of this generally accepted view. It is significant that it is Theseus whom he chooses as his speaker. Theseus speaks of God, "the first mover," creating love:

> For with that faire cheyne of love he bond
> The fyr, the eyr, the water, and the lond
> In certeyn boundes, that they may nat flee.[10]

The bond of love is thus divinely created and serves as a unifying force. Marriage confirms and sanctifies this love. This is what true love is, deep and enduring love which is perfectly conscious of its social relevance and responsibilities. It had not only a moral and social impact, but was considered so holy that marriage was a religious institution:

> Marriage had assumed not only a positive social value, but various spiritual symbols were found in it. The meeting of God and the soul, the relation of the Church and Christ, these also involved bonds which were described in marital terms.[11]

(iii) A very serious view of "blind love" has been taken by Frank Kermode. First of all he explains the theme of blind love as it has been expounded in the play. The four Athenians are all examples of this blind love. It is introduced in the very first scene. Kermode observes:

> Love-fancy as bred in the eye is called a kind of doting, this is held to end in disasters of the kind that over-took Adonis, Romeo, Pyramus.[12]

The fate of Pyramus and Thisby as presented by the mechanicals shows this "disastrous end of doting of love brought to confusion" and the emotion engendered by this masque is "a comic equilibrium." This blind love is expounded in various ways throughout the play. Puck is a natural force, a mischievous Cupid who produces blind dotage for the juice he uses is as efficient as Cupid's arrows. When the antidote is used then all of them, Titania and Bottom included, come to their senses. The experience of the night seems to be a dream.

Frank Kermode then focusses his attention on the word "dream". The play purports to be the dream of a midsummer night. What kind of dream is it? There are five kinds of dreams as given by Macrobius in his *The Dream of Scipio*. The kind of dream that the Athenians and Titania have had is known as "phantasma", i.e., a dream that does not have any meaning.

It is Bottom's dream, however, which is the most important. It is here that this critic gives an extremely serious interpretation of this blind love. He turns his attention to Bottom's speech and lays special stress on the fact that Bottom is overwhelmed by his dream and is incapable of even talking about it:

> I have had a most rare vision—past the wit of man to say what dream it was. Man is but an ass if he go about to expound this dream... the eye of man hath not heard, the ear of man hath not seen, man's hand is not able to taste, his tongue to conceive nor his heart to report, what my dream was![13]

This is generally taken to be a parody of St. Paul's First Epistle to the Corinthians:

> Eye hath not seen, nor ear heard, neither have entered into the heart of man the thing which God hath prepared for them that love him.[14]

Frank Kermode proceeds to draw a parallel between Bottom's dream and St. Paul's epistle and also the experiences of Apuleius (*vide* the section on the Sources in Ch. 9, *infra*). He says, first of all, that Bottom's dream is by nature different from the dream experienced by the other Athenians and that whereas their dream is a meaningless "Phantasma," Bottom's dream is a "somnium." Such dreams are symbolic dreams, not to be understood unless explained by an interpreter. Bottom's dream, then, is a highly significant dream—it is a dream of divine love.

It is what St. Paul says: the things that God hath prepared for them that love him." Bottom's dream is of the love of Titania, a supernatural entity. Kermode says that Bottom, St. Paul and Apuleius, all of these three have something in common:

> What they have in common is transformation, and an experience of divine love. Bottom has known the love of the triple goddess in a vision.[15]

This kind of vision or dream is something that cannot be explained, therefore the term "blind love" can be applied to it, with a totally different meaning:

> This is the contrary interpretation of blind love; the love of God or Isis, a love beyond the power of the eyes.[16]

This is how, according to Kermode, blind love, in different senses, is the theme of the play. This very serious, even religious, interpretation, is quite controversial. Not all critics would agree. The *Dream* is usually taken as a light-hearted comedy and this view is too heavy for it. The late nineteenth century critic, J.O. Halliwell-Phillipps had cautioned against this kind of treatment:

> A Midsummer Night's Dream is too exquisite a composition to be dulled by the influence of philosophical analysis.[17]

(B) THE THEME OF INCONSTANCY

This theme, like the ones explained above, is also based on the theme of love but is still slightly different. Those which have been mentioned above are concerned with the nature of love, but this theme is more concerned with the persons who are in love, i.e., with the characters. It is, in other words, more concrete in nature than those theories that have already been discussed and which are comparatively more abstract.

Peter G. Phialas, expounding this theory, thinks that Shakespeare has always been pre-occupied with the theme of inconstancy and constancy in love:

> The theme of inconstancy in love, the violation of vows offered in the hyperbolical idiom of romantic lovers, lay

close to the centre of Shakespeare's dramatic consciousness.[18]

This theme is to be found in each of his comedies, from the earliest to the last, in various different ways. Here in the *Dream* we have a serious as well as comic treatment of it and both constancy and inconstancy are to be found. The story of Theseus and Hippolyta provide a framework. Theseus had many love-affairs in the past. Oberon mentions them when accusing Titania of pratiality towards Theseus:

> Didst thou not lead him through the glimmering night
> From Periguna, whom he ravished,
> And make him with fair Aegles break his faith
> With Ariadne and Antiopa?[19]

Four love-affairs are mentioned here. This is not all, for according to the best-known version of the Theseus myth, he had married Phaedra, who was Ariadne's sister, though here Shakespeare marries him to Hippolyta (*vide* Sources, Ch. 9, *infra*).

Prior to Hippolyta, then, he had already had five love-affairs (or four if we go by this text only). In other words he has been an inconstant lover. Now, however, he has taken on the responsibilities of a king. He is going to marry Hippolyta and be an example to the rest of the kingdom. He describes his wedding-day as:

> The sealing-day between my love and me
> For everlasting bond of fellowship.[20]

He thus changes from inconstancy to constancy. As his former affairs have not been depicted in the play he stands as a pattern of ideal love.

This is not the case with the others. The four Athenians as well as the royal fairy couple provide examples of inconstant love. The couple which first enter the forest, Hermia and Lysander, are deeply in love with each other. They protest their love in strong terms, Lysander plans the elopement and marriage and Hermia affirms her love:

> I swear to thee by Cupid's strongest bow,

By his best arrow with the golden head
By the simplicity of Venus's doves
By that which knitteth souls and prospers loves.[21]

This is emphatic enough. Then we see them in Act II, sc. ii in which Lysander says:

Love takes the meaning in Love's conference.
I mean that my heart unto yours is knit,
So that but one heart we can make of it;
Two bosoms interchained with another
So then two bosoms and a single troth.[22]

It is most ironical that in the same scene, in line lll, he changes his allegiance completely. As soon as he and Hermia have fallen asleep, Puck comes and drips the juice into his eyes and he sees Helena on waking up. So, a mere sixty lines later, he expresses his love for her in extravagant terms:

And run through fire I will for thy sweet sake!
Transparent Helena![23]

So Helena has now got an unwanted suitor and he regards his love for Hermia as mere childish infatuation which he has outgrown:

Content with Hermia? No; I do repent
The tedious minutes I with her have spent.
Not Hermia, but Helena I love.[24]

This love is an artificially induced one, but the effects are, all the same, excruciating ones for all the persons concerned. Then just as dramatically as he fell in love, so, after his eyelids have been doctored, he veers off towards Hermia once more.

Demetrius offers an example which is hardly better. It is told by Lysander that at one time he had been in love with Helena and has now changed over to Hermia (which is the root of all the confusions and heart-burnings in the play). This had, just like Theseus's love-affairs, happened before the play had opened. So, in the forest he spurns Helena and leaves her alone in the darkness (Act II sc. i). Then once more the supernatural agents interfere and he falls out of love with Hermia and in love with Helena. He is puzzled:

I wot not by what power
(But by some power it is) my love to Hermia
Melted as melts the snow...
... ...
And all the faith, the virtue of my heart
The object and the pleasure of mine eye.
Is only Helena.[25]

It is taken for granted that this love will continue, in all its fervour, like Lysander's and Theseus's, for the rest of his life, for ever.

When we come to Titania and Oberon, we see that Titania is out of harmony with Oberon. Then she is made to fall in love with Bottom. When she is disenchanted she once more becomes the loving spouse of Oberon.

Thus, throughout the play, the pattern of changing alliances in love weave a design of light and shadow. Some of it has been there in the nature of the characters themselves and some have been induced by supernatural agencies. The play let is the only instance of total constancy, though presented comically:

> Thus, then, was Shakespeare's point of departure how to treat in a fresh but comprehensive way that particular aspect of his great theme of love .... Here in this play Shakespeare presents the theme of inconstancy in love in a comic mode.[26]

(C) THEME OF METAMORPHOSIS

This is one of the most recent views of the theme, held and expounded by Cedric Watts. According to him, all the characters in the play undergo transformations or metamorphoses, and this transformation is the central theme:

> So this play is about metamorphoses, "translation," transformations ... metamorphoses are at work in our mental filling-systems, logic takes a holiday.[27]

Each of the characters undergoes, a metamorphosis. He argues that the deity presiding over the entire play is the Moon-Goddess or Diana who is constantly changing. So changes or metamorphoses occur throughout the play. The young lovers, who seem to be devoted to each other change, albeit briefly, into angry, jealous and quarrelsome people, and then change back again. Theseus is changed from a young, thoughtless lover into a responsible king. Even as a king he changes, for in the first scene he seems to abide by the age-old rules of Athens, preserving the tradition of his realm:

> Or else the law of Athens yields you up
> (Which by no means we may extenuate)
> To die, or to a vow of single life.[28]

Yet, at the end of the play, he easily sways, not only the ancient laws of Athens aside, but the parental authority of Egeus as well:

> Egeus, I will overbear your will;
> For in the temple, by and by, with us,
> These couples shall eternally be knit.[29]

Not only Theseus, but Hippolyta is also metamorphosed from a warlike Amazon to a loving wife. The rules of Athens themselves change from inflexible laws into something so trivial that they can he ignored. In the playlet all the comic characters are changed into mythical figures and even the moon itself changes into a lantern. Thus the play rings various changes on the theme of metamorphoses of many different kinds.

(D) WAKING VS. VISIONS

It is the view of G.K. Chesterton that, first of all the *Dream* is the greatest of Shakespeare's comedies and he sums up the theme of the play twice in the course of his essay on it. It is not that he calls it a theme as such, but his meaning is quite clear:

> The whole question which is balanced, and balanced nobly and fairly, in *A Midsummer Night's Dream* is whether the life of waking or the life of the vision, is the real life, the *sine qua non* of man.[30]

Throughout his analysis of the play he lays emphasis on the importance of dream in it. Indeed, it can be seen that the element of dream is truly very important in it and the idea is given special emphasis towards the end. Plotting to bring all misunderstandings to an end, Oberon tells Puck how to set it about so that:

> When they next wake, all this derision
> Shall seem a dream and fruitless vision.[31]

Again, in the next scene Oberon tells Puck to take the ass-head away from Bottom so that he may go back to Athens with all the others:

> And think no more of this night's accidents
> But as the fierce vexation of a dream.[32]

A few lines later Titania wakes up and thinks of her infatuation for Bottom to have been a dream:

> My Oberon! What visions have I seen!
> Methought I was enamoured of an ass.[33]

But Oberon points to the sleeping Bottom and so makes her realize that she had really been in love with him. She is an immortal and cannot be, indeed, should not be, deceived. But the other characters are not put in the right. Demetrius, puzzled, asks the others:

> But are you sure
> That we are now awake? It seems to me,
> That yet we sleep, we dream.[34]

Yet the audience knows that the events that had taken place during the night are true, though these characters will never know this. For the moment they are wondering whether they are asleep or awake, whether what had happened in the night is true and the life of the morning is a dream or not. But as time passes the night's doings will become more and more vague in their mind, they will think them to have really been only dreams.

The same happens to Bottom when he awakes. He however does not have any doubts—he is sure that he had had a dream and decides to make a ballad out of it. Perhaps this is because his experience had been so other-worldly that it cannot be believed to be true. The lovers' changes of loyalty are possible, but the love of the Fairy Queen for a man like Bottom is plumb incredible.

And we fairies, that do run
By the triple Hecate's team
From the presence of the sun
Follow darkness like a dream.[35]

Then comes the well-known epilogue and Puck describes the story as a dream:

And this weak and idle theme
No more yielding but a dream.[36]

There are, thus, several levels of meaning involved here. The events of the night are true, but thought to be dreams and the entire play is itself a dream. Chesterton imagines the fairies coming in at the end, and, looking at the audience, saying to themselves:

Suppose we are the reality and they are the shadows.[37]

This is very imaginative, but not many critics will agree with it. The experiences in the forest are so intense that they are confused with real life. This reminds one of Keats's ecstasy in *Ode to a Nightingale*. At the end of the poem there is doubt in the poet's mind whether this world is the real one or the world of imagination where he had withdrawn. In the case of our play only the audience knows the truth and the fairies.

It can thus be seen that the theme of the play, though it is generally taken to be the theme of love, is still capable of many different interpretations. The *Dream* is a comparatively simple play and has not given rise to as many interpretations as other plays have, but the very fact that just one theme has given rise to so many variations points to its complexity.

REFERENCES

1. Fluchère, *op. cit.*, p. 195.
2. Charlton, *op. cit.*, p. 108.
3. Act I, sc. i., ll. 128-31, p. 36.
4. Charlton, *op. cit.*, p. 117.
5. Act I, sc. i., ll. 16-17, p. 33.
6. Act V, sc. i., ll. 387-404, p. 93.
7. Charlton, *op. cit.*, p. 120.
8. Act III, sc. i., ll. 131-132, p. 58.

9. Dent, R.W., Imagery in *A Midsummer Night's Dream,* in Price, A; *op. cit.*, p. 127.
10. Skeat, W.W., ed., *The Canterbury Tales,* New York, The Modern Library, 1957, p. 85.
11. Olson, Paul A., *The Meaning of Court Marriage,* in Price, A., *op. cit.*, p. 78.
12. Kermode, Frank, *Shakespeare's Best Comedy,* in Price, A., *op. cit.*, p. 115.
13. Act IV, sc. i., ll. 203-211, pp. 79-80.
14. I, Corinthians, 2:9. *The Holy Bible,* New York, American Bible Society, n.d., p. 170.
15. Kermode, *op. cit.*, p. 118.
16. *Ibid.*
17. Price, A., *op. cit.*, p. 40.
18. Phialas, Peter G., *Shakespeare's Romantic Comedies: The Development of their Form and Meaning,* Chapel Hill, The University of N. Carolina Press, 1966, p. 106.
19. Act II, sc. i., ll. 77-80, p. 45.
20. Act I, sc. i., ll. 84-85, p. 35.
21. Act I, sc. i., ll. 169-72, p. 37.
22. Act II, sc. ii., ll. 54-58, pp. 51-52.
23. Act II, sc. ii., ll. 111-12, p. 53.
24. Act II, sc. ii., ll. 119-21, p. 53.
25. Act IV, sc. i., ll. 163-70, p. 78.
26. Phialas, P.G., *op. cit.*, p. 105.
27. Watts, C., *op. cit.*, pp. 11-14.
28. Act I, sc. i., ll. 119-21, p. 36.
29. Act IV, sc. i., ll. 178-80, p. 79.
30. Price, A., *op. cit.*, p. 43.
31. Act III, sc. ii., ll. 370-71, p. 71.
32. Act IV, sc. i., ll. 67-68, p. 75.
33. Act IV, sc. i., ll. 75-76, p. 76.
34. Act IV, sc. i., ll. 191-93, p. 79.
35. Act V, sc. i., ll. 367-70, p. 92.
36. Act V, sc. i., 412-13, p. 93.
37. Price, A., *op. cit.*, p. 44.

7

The Major Characters

SHAKESPEARE'S CHARACTERS

Drama as has been recognized from ancient days, is the "imitation of life, image of truth, mirror of custom" and what can best fulfill all these requirements if not the characters of a play? In this sphere our poet stands unrivalled. His characters are much more than realistic and three-dimensional persons, for they often gain symbolic dimensions, thus growing into universal figures. There are some (Marlowe being a notable example) who depict their central figures with great expertise, but other characters are neglected. Shakespeare, except in his early works (to which our presents play belongs), depicts all characters in such a way that they attain an individual status.

It also has to be remembered that he has given more memorable dramatic characters than anyone else. The great tragic heroes like Macbeth, Hamlet *et al.*, the heroines of comedies like Rosalind, Viola *et al.* and many others are immortal figures. Other dramatists have given one or two, but he has given an entire gallery of such portraits.

Moreover, he never reached a point of stagnation. There is continuous development in his career. His understanding of human beings developed as he himself grew older and so did his capacity of depicting characters. Pope's comment on his psychological insight, given two centuries ago, still holds true:

> His characters are so much Nature herself that, tis a sort of injury to call them by so distant a name as copies of her.[1]

This expertise, however, was not there in the beginning. It was acquired with painstaking observation and inborn intuition. In the first phase he was learning his art and the characters show signs of immaturity. The witty lords of *Love's Labour's Lost* can be but barely distinguished from one another though even at this stage Lord Berowne stands out. In he present play there is Bottom, one of his first memorable characters.

The second phase shows more conscious artistry in every field, including that of characterization. It is here that we have the important male figures of the chronicle plays and the captivating heroines, Rosalind, Beatrice, Portia and Viola become so important that their male counterparts pale into insignificance. The only male character of these comedies who towers above everyone else is Shylock, a controversial figure of gigantic proportions.

The great tragic heroes belong to the third stage of his career. The four great tragedies and the problem comedies were written at this time, presenting a world in which evil predominates. The great figures of Hamlet, Othello, Lear and Macbeth were created at this time. Among memorable female figures there is lady Macbeth who will be an outstanding figure by any standard.

We find a different kind of human beings in the last Romances. These characters obtain an almost religious dimension. The chief character undergoes a spiritual journey. He commits sins and then expiates them by long years of suffering and repentance and finally gains forgiveness. Meanwhile a purer and more innocent younger generation has grown to maturity, to carry on the business of life and preparation.

Shakespeare, though he had astounding originality, did not create his characters entirely out of his own imagination. Contemporary stage-conventions and philosophical concepts provided a base, as well as classical rules and examples. Rules for characterization had been laid down by Aristotle, expounded and exemplified by later critics. As has been pointed out earlier, he had studied classical plays in his school days, the plays of Plautus, Terence and Seneca *(vide* ch. 3, Life and Works, *supra).*

There were also many other works that defined and gave examples of characters, Like Newton's *The Touchstone of Complexions*, Bishop Hall's *Characters of Virtues and Vices*, Sir Thomas Overbury's *Characters,* etc. When in need of a certain kind of character, the dramatists could turn to these.

Theophrastus has given more than a hundred of such character-sketches. The tradition had been started by Aristotle who gave sketches of many characters in his *Nichomachaean Ethics*. In *Poetics* he also laid down certain rules, applicable to all dramatic characters, irrespective of the fact whether they were tragic characters or comic ones. There are four traits all characters should have: (a) Proportion or goodness, (b) Appropriateness, (c) Realism and (d) Consistency.

The first of these, the quality of proportion (often translated as Goodness), has two implications. The moral intention underlying any action or speech must be good:

> Any speech or action that manifests moral purpose of any kind will be expressive of character: the character will be good if the purpose is good.[2]

This goodness, however, is a relative goodness, differing with characters of different classes. If a servant, says Aristotle, refrains from theft then he is good but the same quality does not signify any very remarkable goodness in a gentleman. This concept was later extended to include the possibility of evil in a character. Goodness and evil must both exist in a character just as they do in human beings.

The second quality is Appropriateness or propriety. A character should act or speak in accordance with the kind of person that he is:

> There is a type of manly valour; but valour in a woman, or unscrupulous cleverness, is inappropriate.[3]

This rule is faithfully followed. Even in the *Dream,* early work as it is, the actions and speeches of the characters are true to their personality, as will be apparent when they are analysed.

Realism is the third quality demanded by Aristotle. Characters should be true to life. Aristotle carefully points out that this quality is different from goodness and propriety, but he does not say much else about it. Shakespeare's characters, indeed, are always true to life. Their actions and speeches never go against what is perfectly natural and realistic. This realism is seen at its best in our play in the portrayal of the comic characters.

Above all the other qualities, however, there is the fourth quality of consistency. This demands that the character should remain true to his own inner nature and must not change drastically. Here, as far as our play is concerned, it might be said that the manner in which the two young men fall in and out of love is proof of inconsistency. This objection is not valid, because, however inconsistent and drastic these changes may be, they are brought about by supernatural agents and are unavoidable.

The delineation of characters, thus, depends on two important factors. On the theoretical side there are the classical rules and on the practical side there are the character-sketches given by the classical and the contemporary writers. These were available to everyone, yet it is Shakespeare who has given us characters who have become part of our lives. He did not defy the age-old rules and contemporary customs. Instead, very often, he turned them to his own advantage. Henri Fluchère points out:

> It is equally undeniable that, allowing for his own peculiar genius, he conforms with he accepted convention of character-drawing as with other convention.[4]

A valuable classification of his characters is given by L.S. Champion. According to him Shakespeare depicts characters at the level appropriate to the story he is telling. The characters in his comedies suit the action of the play. If the play is such that the stress is more on action or narration than on the character (as in the early comedies like *The Comedy of Errors,* the *Dream,* etc.) then the characters are sketchily drawn. In the later comedies the attention is focussed upon the characters, their "spiritual catharsis" (as in the last Romances), and not so much upon action. Champion, accordingly, divides his characters into three categories. The first of them is:

> The characters who is delineated only on the level of "physical action," never inviting our response to him as an independent individual.[5]

When we turn to the characters of this play, we see first of all, a drawback in the sense that the characters in it are not well-defined, strongly delineated ones. Except for Theseus and Bottom, there is hardly a character who merits serious attention. H.B. Charlton, indeed, has unequivocally asserted:

> Technically, the weakest part of the play is its characterization.[6]

There have been attempts to explain this weakness in terms of dramaturgy. L.S. Champion, for example, accepts the play as a "situation comedy" *(vide* Ch. 4, *supra).* In such plays the stress falls on the action or the situations created by the action. The characters are manipulated to suit the different situations. As a result, they are often sketchily drawn:

> The Athenian quartet are basically static characters manipulated into humorous contrasts and incongruities. Indeed, they are virtually caricatures of lovesick youth.[7]

These opinions express the general view of the level of excellence in the art of characterization mostly negative in nature. About the range and the variety of the characters depicted, however, there can be no two opinions. Except for *The Tempest,* no other play contains a greater variety of characters, for we have superhuman as well as human characters here, and many gradations in both. On the supernatural level, we have the highest social level in the king and the queen. Pluck can be taken as a high level fairy, for he is always accompanying Oberon. He has to do the king's bidding, but he does not belong to the working class like, for example, the fairy he meets in the beginning of the second Act. The four fairies attending the queen are all courtiers. Thus though the fairies are taken from the aristocratic class, there is gradation among them.

Among the humans, likewise, characters are taken from many social levels. At the top of the social ladder are Theseus and Hippolyta. At a lower level are courtiers like Philostrate who is the master of Revels. Slightly lower (because he is not a regular courtier) is Egeus who definitely belongs to the aristocracy. No titles are attached to his name in the list of *Dramatis Personae,* but Hermia refers to him as "his lordship" and Theseus addresses him familiarly. The lovers also belong to the same social level.

Then, with the mechanicals, we come to the working class-weavers, joiners, tailors, etc. They are sturdy, loyal citizens, humble in the presence of royalty, but full of self-respect. G.M. Trevelyan has told us that though class barriers existed, they were not resented in the Elizabethan age. Every man got a respectable payment for an honest day's labour and thus had independence and self-respect *(vide* Ch. 2, The Socio-political Background, *supra).*

This great variety of characters have been contrasted and manipulated with great artistry. They have been as a whole, called "bizarrely diverse" and listing the various categories, C. Watts say:

> Early in *Midsummer Night's Dream,* social and conceptual hierarchies are firmly established.[8]

A serious interpretation of the characters in the *Dream* has been given by Stephen Fender. The characters, according to him, are morally ambivalent. First of all, he points out that it is as if the poet has put a label on each of his characters and depicted him accordingly:

> In *Midsummer Night's Dream*...Shakespeare defines his characters according to what they represent, according to their labels.[9]

In other words this means that the characters are more or less flat and one-dimensional. He explains his meaning by taking the example of the four Athenians. They are "lovers" and so they will behave according to the definition of that word.

In like manner "Puck" is the general term applied to mischievous fairies or goblins, so Puck of the play (whose name is Robin Goodfellow) behaves according to the definition of his name.

This, however, is not all for Shakespeare continually introduces many variations in his depiction of these characters, particularly a moral one and this contains ambivalence:

> ... the ideas and forces which Shakespeare makes his characters (and even locales) represent are in every case morally ambivalent.[10]

All the characters in the play, whether human or fairy, are presented in such a way as to make it clear that they have the potentiality for goodness as well as evil. Puck is a mischievous fairy who worries the housewives by playing tricks on them and puts an ass-head on Bottom. Yet in the play he serves to bring the lovers together by dripping the love-juices on them. The mistake he makes at first by confusing the lovers is an inadvertent one, made through ignorance, not ill-will. Each of the characters can be interpreted from this point of view. Lysander for example is a devoted lover, yet, changed by the love-juice he spurns Hermia and quarrels with Demetrius. Demetrius, on the other hand, spurns Helena and leaves her alone in the forest, but the potentiality for goodness is there in him which is brought out by the love-juice. Theseus had been an irresponsible lover who had abandoned his sweethearts, but now he is a good king. There is this kind of ambivalence in each character.

Usually the characters of this play are divided into three groups: (1) the Athenians, (2) the fairies, (3) the mechanicals. Alexander Leggatt, however, categorises them into four divisions:

> ... and throughout the play, we see four different groups of characters the lovers, the clowns, the older Athenians and the fairies—each group pre-occupied with its own limited problems and largely unaware of the others.[11]

This means that he divided the Athenians into two groups, with the older Athenians, Theseus, Hippolyta and Egeus making up one group. Leggatt says that the groups are largely unaware of the others, but this is scarcely true. Oberon is very aware of the young lovers, and so is Egeus. The mechanicals exist in the play precisely because they are so aware of the aristocratic characters. They are all unaware of the fairies, but otherwise the groups are fully aware of each other.

Let us now turn to the characters themselves. The aristocratic characters, except for Philostrate, shall be treated as major characters. Bottom also, despite his humble position in society, is a major character, for he is one of the best-delineated characters in the early plays. The fairies shall be treated as major characters as well, but in a separate group.

(a) Theseus

Theseus is actually a mythical character, one of the Greek heroes, like Hercules, Perseus or Bellerophon. There are many stories about him. In this play Shakespeare has presented him as an ideal king. He comes only briefly in the play, in the first scene, part of the first scene of Act IV, and in the last scene yet, Charlton says:

> Theseus stamps his mind on the play.[12]

This is because he has a mind, a thoughtful, reasonable mind, to be able to stamp it on the play. In the first scene we see him as a man who is eagerly waiting for his fighting and conquering the Amazonian queen is one of the episodes. Now he wants to settle down to rule his subjects as a king, and wants to put his wanderings firmly behind him. Fighting and winning might have glamour, but he realizes that all this must lead to a stable life. He had won Hippolyta by sword, but he wants to sanctify their union properly:

> Hippolyta, I wooed thee with my sword,
> And won thy love, doing thee injuries;
> But I will wed thee in another key,
> With pomp, with triumph and with revelling.[13]

This is to be no clandestine love-affair as so many of his affairs had been. Later in the scene he makes his views on marriage very clear. It is duty of men and women to marry and lead a happy domestic life:

> But, earthlier happy is the rose distilled,
> Than that which, withering on the virgin thorn
> Grows, lives and dies in single blessedness.[14]

He upholds the sanctity not only of marriage but of parental authority in the family:

Be advised, fair maid,
To you, your father should be as a god:
One that composed your beauties; yea, and one
To whom you are but as a form in wax.[15]

He shows himself to be a dignified, considerate king who sympathises with both the father and the daughter. Thus in the one and the same our poet shows two different facets of his personality: the lover and the king.

After this the main business of the play begins and we do not see him till the fourth Act. This act shows him towards the end of the first scene. Throughout this fateful night the lovers have wandered about in the forest, falling in and out of love with the two girls. Then with the dawn comes Theseus, bringing the sane, sensible, everyday world with him. He is the character who represents sanity and reason so all enchantments disappear, and ordinary world makes its appearance with him. Drama is an imitation of life and can deal with a midsummer night's dream only for a short time

At first he talks of hunting only and then his attention is drawn by the sleeping lovers. He remembers that this is the day when Hermia has to tell them of her decision. After the lovers have been awakened and have explained their adventures in brief, he quickly takes the decision of getting them married in the same ceremony which is to solemnize his own nuptials:

In the temple, by and by, with us
These couples shall eternally be Knit.[16]

In this context it should be remembered that to take the right decision, and that, too, quickly, is one of the special abilities of one of the characters sketched by Aristotle, the *megalo-psychia,* or the great-souled man. This is one of the most important characters given by Aristotle and in Shakespeare's own time he appears repeatedly as Mr. Great-Heart, Mr. Nobility, etc. Ben Jonson had written an unfinished elegy on a contemporary, entitled *The Noble Nature*, modelled on this character Aristotle gives many traits of such a man. In the translation given below *megalo-psychia* has been translated as "the proud man". Some of his traits are:

(a) The man is thought to be proud who thinks himself worthy of great things, being worthy of them.

(b) Greatness in every virtue would seem to be characteristic of a proud man.

(c) It is hard to be truly proud, for it is impossible without nobility and goodness of character.

(d) It is chiefly with honours and dishonours that the proud man is concerned.

(e) Proud men are thought to be disdainful.

(f) The proud man despises justly.[17]

These are only a few of the traits given by Aristotle and they are all apt descriptions of Theseus.

We see him next in the last Act. The marriage ceremony is over, they have all enjoyed the royal banquet and now want some entertainment. First, however, comes the famous scene with the speech on the lunatic, the lover and the poet. The lovers have recounted their adventures in the forest and Theseus is very sceptical about the story. According to him lovers are very like madmen for they all have a teeming imagination:

...that apprehend
More than cool reason ever comprehends.[18]

Madmen, lovers and poets, all have strong imagination. The madman sees terrible vision of devils. The lover sees great beauty in his beloved when perhaps she is not beautiful at all. It is Theseus's description of the poet which is the most famous part of this speech and is thought to express Shakespeare's own thoughts.

The poet's eyes, in a fine frenzy rolling,
Doth glance from heaven to earth, from earth to heaven,
And as imagination bodies forth
The form of things unknown, the poet's pen
Turns them to shapes, and gives to airy nothing
A local habitation and a name.[19]

This passage has been explained in many different ways. Learned scholars had explained it with reference to Elizabethan theories of poetry, of inspiration, of imagination, of madness, of love, and of the human soul. Theseus is the representation of sanity and rationality and it is very significant that it is to him that Shakespeare has given the honour of delivering this speech. There are many characters in his plays who write poems, many who are thoughtful, many who are intellectuals (Hamlet has all these three attributes). None of these characters has been given such a serious and memorable passage about the nature and function of poetry. A paraphrase will mean that the poet, with the help of his imagination creates such things as do not really exist. This is the simplest explanation, but the passage is very complex and has multiple layers of meaning that can be understood only with a knowledge of all the theories mentioned above.

Then Theseus turns his attention to the evening's entertainment. Philostrate, his Master of Revels, presents him with a list of available entertainments. He has four of them to choose from and he chooses the one that the mechanicals have been preparing. He is intrigued by the title of the play and asks Philostrate for more information. Philostrate has nothing to say in praise of it:

in all the play
There is not one word apt, one player fitted.[20]

Theseus asks about the players and is told:

Hard-headed men that work in Athens here
Who never laboured in their minds till now;
And now have toiled their unbreathed memories
With this same play, against your nuptials.[21]

Theseus chooses this play and insists on its being performed though Philostrate tries to dissuade him and Hippolyta also is not in favour of it. This is not unreasonable obstinacy, nor is he motivated by a desire to ridicule the players. On the contrary he shows himself as a true and noble king, for he says, never mind if the play is sub-standard: it is the love and loyalty of the players that matter. They are simple artisans, and with much hope and fear have they laboured over this play. One must think of that:

> What poor duty cannot do, noble respect
> Takes it in might, not merit.[22]

He tells Hippolyta how "great clerks," standing up to deliver well-composed welcome speeches, have become tongue-tied in his presence but he never took any offence, for he understood their condition:

> Trust me, sweet.
> Out of this silence yet I picked a welcome;
> ....
> Love therefore and tongue-tied simplicity,
> In least, speak most to my capacity.[23]

It has been thought that these lines were written as a special compliment to Queen Elizabeth.[24] In this wonderful speech Theseus reveals himself as a true gentleman, courteus and considerate. The fairies had made fun of the poor humble artisans but Theseus does not:

> Theseus (even if he later laughs at the show) here gives the immortals a moral lesson.... It is one of those little speeches which help—albeit tricklingly and imperceptibly, to make the world a better place.[25]

Then, as the play proceeds, he as well as the courtiers comment upon the play, but it is done most good-naturedly. There is never any demoralising satire in his own comments and the court follows his lead. Thus, after the Wall, presented by Snout, makes a speech, the following comments are made:

> Theseus: Would you desire: lime and hair to speak better?
>
> Demetrius: It is the wittiest partition that ever I heard discourse, my lord.[26]

He enjoys the show thoroughly and when Starveling the tailor comes with a lantern in his hand, saying that the lantern is the moon and he himself the man in the moon, Theseus says:

> This is the greatest error of all the rest: the man should be put into the lantern. How is it else the man in the moon?[27]

Hippolyta is bored by the play but Theseus, administering a mild rebuke, says:

> ... but yet, in courtesy, in all reason we must stay the time.[28]

This is truly a lesson in courtesy. Theseus is an example to all rulers, even in this small detail. Not only does he stay, but he encourages the players as well ("Well run, Thisby," "Well moused, Lion"). When the play comes to an end he boosts the morale of the players by saying: " Your play needs no excuse." He is a noble and magnanimous king.

Theseus is thus portrayed as a noble and good king, worthy to be called a Great-Souled man as given by Aristotle. This character had been depicted by Overbury and Plutarch mainly as a warrior and a lover. Chaucer had depicted him as a noble king and our poet has followed Chaucer most faithfully racher than the classical authors (*Vide* Ch. 9, the section on Sources, *infra)*. He is generally taken as the purveyor of the rational common-sense view of the world and of man's nature. Chesterton calls him "the incarnation of a happy and generous rationalism."[29]

A parallel has been drawn between Theseus, Oberon and Bottom. All three are forceful persons, standing out independently. They are all rulers. Theseus and Oberon are kings over men and fairies respectively and Bottom is easily the most outstanding among all the artisans. Theseus stands out by virtue of his rationality as well as his generous acceptance of the faults of his fellow human beings:

> Set between the two kings Bottom and Oberon, himself a mightier king than they, he is master of all that is best in either.[30]

(b) Lysander

Lysander is loved by Hermia but rejected by her father. Why Egeus does not want him as a son-in-law is a mystery. Lysander himself clarifies the position to Theseus. In wealth and rank he is equal to Demetrius and, moreover, is Hermia's chosen lover. Also, as he points out, Demetrius had a love affair with Helena and has now shifted his allegiance to Hermia, though Helena still loves him. As a romantic lover, thus, Lysander is ideal. He wooes Hermia in the approved courtly manner, serenading her, writing poems and sending gifts as Egeus complains:

> Thou, thou Lysander; thou hast given her rhymes,
> And interchanged love-token with my child;
> Thou hast, by moonlight, at her window sung,
> With feigning voice, verses of faining love.[31]

This is the time-worn method of courtly love. Silvia in *The Two Gentlemen of Verona* had been serenaded, and, a few years later, Orlando will write poems to Rosalind.

He and Hermia are, like Romeo and Juliet, or like Pyramus and Thisby, star-crossed lovers. He has no other option but to elope with Hermia. It seems that he has spent quite some thought over their situation, for, when the time demands it, he has a ready-made plan. He shows himself to be a resourceful and determined young man. Literary critics have often declared that the two lovers lack individuality and can hardly be distinguished from each other. This is not the case at all. It is true that he talks in the stilted ornate diction of a romantic lover but he is a sensible young man determined to get his way.

It has been objected that elopement is not a socially approved course of action. This is perfectly true but desperate diseases need desperate remedies. They will lose each other forever if they bow down to social strictures. Elopement is forced upon them. What is more, they will go to his aunt's house and then get married, so impropriety will be kept to a minimum.

He shows an error of judgement when Helena comes and he takes her into his confidence. He does not dream that she will betray them at once.

We see him in the second scene of Act II, by which time he and Hermia are tired and have also lost their way. They decide to lie down and rest. When Hermia wants that he should not lie near her, at first he objects, but then yields to persuasion, showing himself as an amenable and reasonable youth. This, however, leads to their undoing for when he awakes after his eyes have been doctored by Puck, it is Helena he sees and not Hermia. He promply falls in love with her. If Shakespeare had been poking fun at courtly love the laughter becomes far more pronounced, the language becomes more emphatic:

> And run through fire I will, for thy sweet sake
> Transparent Helena! Nature shows art
> That through thy bosom makes me see thy heart.
> Where is Demetrius? O how fit a word
> Is that vile name to perish on my sword.[32]

He tries to rationalize this sudden and violent change of front, professing his love for Hermia to have been a folly. Helena, of course, takes all this in very bad part, thinking it to be a cruel joke on her. Lysander is in dead earnest and determines "to honour Helena and to be her knight." This is the reason the critics talk of "love-blindness" and "love-madness."

Then Demetrius, in his turn, falls in love with Helena and becomes Lysander's rival. The juice has turned both of them into highly aggressive persons. Lysander had not, up till now, shown any aggressive qualities but now he is raring for a fight. He abuses and shakes off Hermia:

> Hang off, thou cat, thou bur ! Vile thing, let loose;
> Or I will shake thee from me like a serpent.[33]

Such behaviour is undreamt of in any young man from a good family, but this is what the juice has done to him.

Lured by Puck, he soon falls asleep and once more the juice is dripped on his eyes and *status quo* is restored. He is half asleep and dazed on waking up, but he pulls himself together and it is he who gives Theseus an account of what has happened:

> My lord, I shall reply amazedly
> Half asleep, half waking. But as yet I swear
> I cannot truly say how I come here.[34]

His ability to interact with others is seen when in Act V sc. i he answers the congratulations of Theseus with fitting good-will while Demetrius remains silent. He is definitely more vocal than the other.

Lysander as well as Demetrius have been systematically neglected by literary critics. They are always mentioned together, as if they had no separate individuality. Yet they are different from each other. At the same time it has to be granted that the delineation has not been done carefully, for, though they are the heroes of the play, yet they are comic figures, manipulated by the fairies. So the poet has kept the tone very light. There is one critic, H. Woelffel, who has taken the lovers seriously and his opinion of Lysander is given quite clearly:

> ...in Lysander the poet wished to represent a noble magnanimous nature sensitive to the charms of the loveliness of soul and of spiritual beauty.[35]

(c) Demetrius

Whatever has been said about Lysander is partially true of Demetrius also. He, like Lysander, is the romantic lover of the play. If Lysander and Hermia are compared with Romeo and Juliet respectively as star-crossed lovers then Demetrius is comparable to Paris—suitor of a girl who repulses him. He is favoured by the father, but this is of no avail. He is also less vocal than Lysander. In the first scene for example he speaks only two lines. After this we see him in Act II, sc. i when he comes to the forest in pursuit of the runaway lovers. He is a perfect gentleman also, as becomes evident when he rebukes Helena for following him and she replies "Your virtue is my privilege". She knows him for a gentleman.

After this he comes on the stage after a long interval in Act III sc. ii. He has succeeded in finding Hermia who has by now been forsaken by Lysander. When he sees that Hermia is determined to spurn him, he lies down to rest and it is then that Oberon drips the juice upon his eyelids. On waking he sees Helena in front of him and falls in love with her:

> O Helena, goddess, nymph, perfect, divine!
> To what, my love, shall I compare thine eyne.[36]

No wonder Helena thinks this abrupt change to be a mockery.

A violent quarrel ensues among the four of them and Demetrius is the first to draw his sword. Then, like Lysander, he is misled and bemused by Puck and lies down to rest. When he wakes, things have become normal between Lysander and Hermia and so his newly-awakened love for Helena helps to bring about the desired end of comedy.

When Egeus tells him that he had stopped Hermia from eloping, that he shall therefore have her for his wife, he speaks in a most sensible manner:

> My good lord, I wot not by what power
> (But by some power it is), my love to Hermia
> Melted as melts the snow...
> ... ...
> The object and the pleasure of mine eye,
> Is only Helena. To her, my lord
> Was I betrothed, ere I saw Hermia.[37]

He now wants nothing better than to marry her. We have the impression that his love, though juice-induced, is true love and will endure.

Of the four of them, he is the only one who has some inkling of what has really happened, for he is the one who suspects "some power" to have been playing with them for some unknown reason and cannot bring himself to believe that they are really awake now:

> But are you sure
> That we are now awake? It seems to me
> That yet we sleep, we dream[38]

As had happened with Lysander, Shakespeare has poked fun at Demetrius also. Moreover, as has been argued by P.G. Phialas, if the theme of the play is inconstancy of love, then he illustrates the theory far better than Lysander does. Lysander had been in love with Hermia and ends the play in the same condition. The inconstancy he had shown had been induced by the fairies. Demetrius however had formerly been betrothed to Helena and then he fell in love with Hermia. This love had come naturally, it had not been produced artificially. In comparison his love for Helena, though intense, is artificial. Perhaps it is this feature that has made the German critic H. Woelffel so harsh:

> ...in Demetrius he has given us
> a nature fundamentally less noble;
> in its final analysis, even unlovely;
> and sensitive only to the impression
> of physical beauty.[39]

He bases this stern judgement on the effect the same love-juice of the two different lovers. He posits that the nature of the two lovers is diametrically opposed to each other, and argues that Shakespeare himself has pointed this out by effect of the juice upon them:

> The effect of the same magical juice on the two men is that Demetrius is rendered faithful, Lysander unfaithful—an incontrovertible sign that their natures, like their affections, are diametrically opposite.[40]

This, however, does not necessarily mean that Demetrius is a less noble character than Lysander as this critic argues. It can easily be said that Lysander had the possibility of inconstancy in his nature which is brought out by the juice and Demetrius had the seeds of constancy within himself which is brought out by the same love-juice.

(d) Hermia

As with the two male lovers, the heroines also have been rather negligently portrayed. Their personalities do not come home to the reader. This, again, does not mean that they have not been individualised. Quite the opposite in fact, for the poet has taken great pains to differentiate between them, in appearance as well as in the dramatic function. Hermia is dark and petite and Helena is tall and fair. In their love-life also, Hermia is more fortunate than Helena.

In the beginning it seems as though Hermia is a most unfortunate girl. She cannot have the man she wants and the lover she does not want is being thrust upon her. In this matter she has been compared with Juliet on whom Pairs has been thrust though she wants Romeo. Hermia is faced with a terrible choice: either she marries Demetrius or she lives as a virgin priestess of Diana or she dies. No wonder she rails against fate. She chooses to live as a priestess rather than marry Demetrius. Thus she succumbs to fate because it appears that there is nothing else that she can do. As soon as Lysander suggests a practicable alternative she is quick to accept it, as is perfectly natural. Her readiness to elope has been frowned upon and also her defiance of law, by W. Oelchelhauser:

> One of Hermia' s characteristics is her lack of respect for her father... as also her pert questions and answers to the duke... behind the Duke's back she snaps her fingers at both of them.[41]

This is a very harsh judgement and is typical of the Victorian Age. Today society has become more lenient. It is also not true that she snaps her fingers at both of the elders, for only after much lamentation does Lysander propose the elopement. She merely agrees to meet him in the forest.

When, after much wanderings in the forest, she comes to know that Lysander has lost the way, she does not upbraid him. Instead she agrees to lie down and rest. She requests him most charmingly and decorously to lie down at a little distance and in spite of his pleadings she is firm in her refusal. This argues that she has a strong sense of propriety.

She is thunderstruck when Lysander tells her that he loves Helena now and not her. She turns against Helena and is quite fierce. She shows no ladylike gentleness and one can easily believe Helena when she says about Hermia:

> She was a vixen when she went to school
> And though she be but little, she is firece.[42]

She is a strong and forceful character and that is the impression she leaves to the last, for after she lies down to sleep beside Lysander she does not speak again, though she is present on the stage.

(e) Helena

Shakespeare has differentiated between his two heroines in

very concrete terms, for they are different from each other in appearance as well as in temperament. Helena is the opposite of Hermia in appearance, being tall as Hermia is petite and fair as Hermia is dark. In her love-life also she is the opposite of Hermia, for Hermia has the love of her beloved, whereas the man Helena wants is devoted to another. She is all the more unfortunate in this because Demetrius was actually betrothed to her and then deserted her for Hermia. She however, cannot be indifferent to him and goes on loving him in spite of everything. This shows great tenacity and endurance in her.

Yet this love has a negative side also, for it is so blind that she betrays the confidence of her friend, Lysander and Hermia. She knows that Demetrius loves Hermia and therefore the sooner she (Hermia) is married to Lysander the better. Yet she goes and tells Demetrius of their elopement, hoping that this will win her favour. This does not happen, as she finds when she follows him to the forest. Her fortunes undergo a drastic change here, for Lysander falls in love with her first and then, soon after, so does Demetrius. Now her situation is exactly what Hermia's had formerly been—she is pursued by two lovers.

Except for the fact that she betrays Lysander and Hermia, there is not much that can be held against her. She shows herself to be, apart from her passionate love for Demetrius, a thoughtful person and also definitely more of a lady than Hermia who in comparison, appears like a shrew. Her treachery, however has been defended by Coleridge:

> The act is very natural; the resolve so to act is, I fear, likewise too true a picture of the lax hold that principles have on the female heart.[43]

She has more depth in her character than Hermia as becomes apparent in the long speech at the end of Act I sc. i, in which she speculates on the nature of love. She hereself is hopelessly, helplessly in love and pronounces several aphorisms:

> Things base and vile, holding no quantity,
> Love can transpose to form and dignity.
> Love looks not with the eyes burt with the mind:
> And therefore is winged Cupid painted blind.[44]

Her nature is far more gentle than that of Hermia, for, as she says later, she is not good at quarrelling. Shakespeare, as a matter of fact, presents a study in contrasts in his presentation of these two heroines. He will present such contrasts in future also, for example in Rosalind and Celia, in Beatrice and Hero, in Viola and Olivia, with one heroine stronger and more assertive than the other.

(f) Bottom

After Theseus, Bottom is clearly the most important character of the play. He is but a hunble weaver, yet he has to be treated as a major character. In fact he is far more important than the Athenian lovers.

His name is indicative of his trade, for he is a weaver, and the word "bottom" means the base of the wooden reel around which thread is wound. He is definitely the leader of the group of artisans. Quince is the director of the playlet, but Bottom is the chief actor without whom the play cannot be staged, as becomes apparent later in the play:

> Flute: If he comes not, then the play is marred. It goes not forward, doth it?
>
> Quince: It is not possible. You have not a man in all Athens able to discharge Pyramus but he.[45]

But this comes towards the end of the play. In the second scene of the first Act, when we see him for the first time, he is portrayed as a self-opinionated man who wants to grab all the roles in the show for himself. He is going to do Pyramus, but he wants to do Thisby and the lion as well. He is sure that he can do it better than anybody else. When he is told that if, doing the lion, he roars too loudly it will be disastrous, he quickly adjust himself:

> I will roar you as gently as any sucking-dove; I will roar an 'twere any nightingale.[46]

This quick adaptability will be of help to him in the fairy-world in accepting Titania's love and the service of the fairy courtiers with aplomb. All the same it shows him up as a man who thinks very highly of himself. Hazlitt remarks:

> He is the most romantic of mechanicals.... He is accordingly represented as conceited, serious and fantasical.[47]

In the rehearsal scenes he is the most dominating person. It is he who suggests the Prologue explaining that Pyramus is not really going to kill himself but that he is not Pyramus at all but Bottom the weaver. It is he who makes the suggestion about the wall. Then he, being Pyramus, opens the play and has to go out. It is then that Puck puts the ass-head on his shoulders, transforming him.

Thereafter, everything is changed. His artisan friends are afraid of him and run off:

> O monstrous! O strange! We are haunted.
> Pray, masters—fly, masters—help![48]

Bottom himself, of course, does not feel any change. He thinks that the others are merely playing a practical joke on him, wanting to frighten him. He sings a song to show he is not frightened, and he is the only human character to sing a song in this play. This song wakes Titania who promptly falls in love with him. It is very significant that Bottom, again, is the only person in the play who can see these fairies. Now, little by little, other qualities of his character are revealed. Though he is a little taken aback at Titania's love for him, he reacts in a very sensible manner:

> Methinks, mistress, you should have little reason for that. And yet, to say the truth, reason and love keep little company together, nowadays. The more the pity.[49]

His hard-headed common sense however cannot get him out of the forest. Instead he is taken deeper into it, into Titania's bower. Before this happens, however, the four attendants of Titania are introduced to him and he behaves like a well-mannered courteous man. He addresses each by name, speaking most politely:

> Bottom: Your name, honest gentleman?
>
> Peaseblossom: (*bows*) Peaseblossom.
>
> B: I pray you, commend me to Mistress
> Squash, your mother and to Master

> Peascod, your father. Good Master pease-
> blossom, I shall desire of you more acquaintance.[50]

This is not fairy language, but it shows not only that Bottom has not lost his head, but that, instead, he is being polite to the best of his ability, but most courteously.

This transformation of Bottom has been understood in many different ways. There is, first of all, a down-to-earth explanation in terms of contemporary situation. The effort of the artisans to put up a play is, of course, a good-nature parody of contemporary theatre and Dr. Johnson has commented on this aspect thus:

> Bottom was perhaps the head of a rival company and is therefore honoured with an Ass's head.[51]

There is a symbolic interpretation as well. According to Renaissance philosophy the ass was the symbol for sensuality:

> ...a fairly accessible interpretation sees it as the symbol for stupidity and sensuality, for the carnal man as opposed to the spiritual.[52]

The most serious view of Bottom has been given by Frank Kermode, who gives a religious version of Bottom's experience. Bottom, on waking up, says:

> I have had a most rare vision. I have had a dream—past the wit of man to say what dream it was. Man is but an ass if he go about to expound this dream...The eye of men hath role not heard, the ear of man hath not seen... what my dream was.[53]

This speech is related to two sources, one classical and the other Biblical. The Biblical allusion is a clear and well-known one, referring to St. Paul's first Epistle to the Corinthians in which he says that God's grace is something that human eyes have not seen and human ears have not heard (*vide* Ch. 6, *supra*).

Apart from this Kermode also refers to Apuleius's famous work *The Golden Ass* in which the hero is transformed into an ass and later, after getting back his original form, he becomes a priest. During the rites of initiation he undergoes many experiences. He is forbidden to speak of these spiritual experiences but says that he had a vision of the Goddess Isis.

Bottom too, like Apuleius's hero undergoes a transformation into an ass and on waking up, like St. Paul and like Lucius he cannot describe these experiences. Kermode concludes that his experience is like the experience of God's grace:

> Bottom is there to tell us that the blindness of love, the domination of the mind over the eye, can be interpreted as a means to grace as well as to irrational animality.[54]

Bottom, on waking up, becomes the same person that he was, and undertakes the staging of the playlet. When the play is being staged and Theseus comments on the Wall, it is Bottom who replies to him, though it is Snout who is the Wall. Again, at the end of the play it is he who addresses the courtly audience and asks if they want the epilogue or not. In other words, he is quite at home in Theseus's palace just as he was in Titania's bower. Indeed, because of his leader-like qualities, G. Wilson Knight has equated him with Theseus and Oberon, and has observed:

> Three persons here have special autonomous existence in their own right, Theseus, Oberon and Bottom. Each is sovereign in his sphere, king over his companions and demands our respect.[55]

Bottom, thus, though a humble artisan, occupies a place with the highest. Even at this early stage Shakespeare has created a memorable character.

REFERENCES

1. Quoted by Fluchère, H., *op. cit.*, p. 131.
2. Butcher, S.H., *Aristotle's Theory of Poetry and Fine Art with a Critical Text Translation of the Poetics,* New Delhi, Kalyani Pubs., 1981, Ch. xv, p. 53.
3. *Ibid.*
4. Fluchère, H., *op. cit.*, p. 136.
5. Champion, L.S., *op. cit.*, p. 8.
6. Charlton, H.B., *op. cit.*, p. 104.
7. Champion, L.S., *op. cit.*, p. 47.

8. Watts, *op. cit.*, p. 11.
9. Fender, S., *Moral Ambivalence* in Price, A., *op. cit.*, p. 146.
10. *Ibid.*, p. 147.
11. Leggatt, A., *Organised Disorder* in Price, A., *op. cit.*, p. 146.
12. Charlton, *op. cit.*, p. 113.
13. Act I, sc. i, ll. 16-19, p. 33.
14. Act I, sc. i, ll. 76-78, p. 35.
15. Act I, sc. i, ll. 46-49, p. 34.
16. Act IV, sc. i, ll. 179-80, p. 79.
17. Mckeon, Richard, ed., *Introduction to Aristotle,* New York, The Modern Library, 1947, pp. 383-88.
18. Act V, sc. i, ll. 5-6, p. 82.
19. Act V, sc. i, ll. 12-17, p. 82.
20. Act V, sc. i, ll. 64-65, p. 83.
21. Act V, sc. i, ll. 72-75, p. 84.
22. Act V, sc. i, ll. 91-92, p. 84.
23. Act V, sc. i, ll. 99-105, pp. 84-85.
24. Brooks, Harold F., ed., *A Midsummer Night's Dream*, London, Methuen, 1979, p. 55.
25. Watts, C., *op. cit.*, pp. 17-18.
26. Act V, sc. i, ll. 164-66, p. 86.
27. Act V, sc. i, ll. 236-38, p. 88.
28. Act V, sc. i, ll. 243-44, p. 89.
29. Chesterton, G.K., in Price, A., *op. cit.*, p. 44.
30. Knight, G.W., *Dissension in Fairyland* in Price, A., *op. cit.*, p. 69.
31. Act I, sc. i, ll. 28-31, p. 34.
32. Act II, sc. ii, ll. 111-115, p. 53.
33. Act III, sc. ii, ll. 260-61, p. 67.
34. Act IV, sc. i, ll. 145-47, p. 78.
35. Price, A., *op. cit.*, p. 35.
36. Act III, sc .ii, ll. 137-38., p. 64.
37. Act IV, sc. i, ll. 163-71, p. 78.
38. Act IV, sc. i, ll. 191-93, p. 79.
39. Price, A., *op. cit.*, p. 35.
40. *Ibid.*
41. *Ibid.*, p. 41.
42. Act III, sc. ii, ll. 324-25, p. 69.

43. Price, A., *op. cit.*, p. 31.
44. Act I, sc. i, ll. 232-35, p. 39.
45. Act IV, sc. ii, ll. 3-6, p. 80.
46. Act I, sc. ii, ll. 71-73, p. 41.
47. Price, A., *op. cit.*, p. 31.
48. Act III, sc. i, ll. 105-06, p. 57.
49. Act III, sc. i, ll. 130-32,p. 58.
50. Act III, sc. i, ll. 170-75, p. 60.
51. Price, A., *op. cit.*, p. 29.
52. Olson, Paul, A., *The Meaning of Court Marriage* in Price, A., *op. cit.*, pp. 86-87
53. Act IV, sc. i, ll. 203-11, pp. 79-80.
54. Kermode, *op. cit.*, p. 118.
55. Knight, G.W., *op. cit.*, p. 68.

8

The Fairies and the Minor Characters

(A) THE FAIRIES

The fairies play an extremely important part in the play. Not only do they provide twists and turns in the plot, they give the comedy an extra dimension—that of the supernatural. The only other play in which Shakespeare makes use of them is *The Tempest.* There, also, directed by Prospero, Ariel brings about all the necessary changes in the plot. As it is, fairies were not anything exotic or alien to Elizabethan imagination. Shakespeare drew upon a rich traditional folklore to create his fairies. Dr. Johnson remarks upon them:

> Fairies in his time were much in fashion; common, tradition had made them, familiar and Spenser had made them great.[1]

Different critics have different views about them. There are four main views, as categorized by Anthony Price. First of all there are those who are not very familiar with English folklore and have read the play in translation. They think that fairies are evil, or, at best amoral. Thus the seventeenth century the German critic G.G. Gervinus says:

> Shakespeare depicts the fairies as creatures devoid of refined feelings and morals... careless and unprincipled themselves, they tempt mortals to be unfaithful.[2]

This is not a readily acceptable view as, first of all, Oberon shows himself capable of refined feelings by sympathising with Helena. He shows magnanimity by wanting and actively trying to make Demetrius fall in love with her. Puck, it is true, makes a mistake in dripping the juice on Lysander's eyelids, but it is not done deliberately. The only piece of mischief is the fixing of the ass-head on Bottom's shoulders but this too is remedied as soon as possible. The fairies are not shown in this play as evil. Instead they are benevolent and come to dance at and bless the triple wedding.

Gervinus is a German critic of the nineteenth century but his attitude is still echoed a century later by Jan Kott who takes a very negative view of the fairies. His interpretation of the Titania-Bottom affair is nauseating. According to him Titania has secret longings for animal love and Puck and Oberon provide this for her by transforming Bottom into an ass-headed monster:

> This is the lover she wanted and dreamed of; only she never wanted to admit it even to herself.[3]

He says much more, none of it positive. It is very necessary for the serious student to know about different critical opinions, but not necessary to agree with them. Jan Kott's is but one opinion among many.

The second school holds that the fairies are not evil. Instead they are benevolent and try to restore peace and harmony in nature and man:

> Their rulers are concerned not with mischief, as traditionally, but with *order* in a quasi-human fashion.[4]

This is perfectly true for, as pointed out, the fairies interfere with the humans for their own good and restore order and harmony. Puck the mischievous fairy is instrumental in bringing about the union of the lovers. He sings:

> Jack shall have Jill;
> Nought shall go ill;
> The man shall have his mare again
> And all shall be well.[5]

This is an opinion with which many critics agree. Katherine Briggs has pointed out how Titania is not only aware of the fact that the quarrel between herself and Oberon has disrupted the natural order, but she even feels concern for the mortals who are affected by it. Even the fact that she has taken a human child away from his proper environment is justifiable as the child is left motherless, and the mother was a friend of hers. She takes the child only because of loyalty to her human friend and because she wants to ensure that he is going to be properly looked after.

This view that the fairies are not malevolent is almost universally accepted and Ernest Schanzer defends them against the allegation of irresponsibility also. It was H.B. Charlton who had accused them of leading a life which was not only free from the cares of domestic life but also, by inference, of being irresponsible and selfish. Instead he (Schenzer) looks upon Oberon and Titania as awe-inspiring figures:

> They are the counterparts in the spirit-world of Theseus and Hippolyta, like them full of stateliness and dignity though more ceremonious and distant.[6]

The third view relates the fairies to the classical gods. According to Walter F. Staton, Jnr., the three main fairies, Oberon, Titania and Puck are like Jupiter, Juno and Mercury. He also points out resemblances between the Titania-Bottom affair and Shakespeare's own narrative poem *Venus and Adonis*. First of all he refers to the classical tales told by Ovid in which the three main characters, according to him, resemble the three main fairies. According to him Oberon, like Jupiter, is "the philandering king who is trying to get away with something." Usually in Ovid's tales Jupiter wants to hold his love-affairs away from Juno's knowledge. Titania, like Juno, is "the jealous and watchful queen" and Puck like Mercury, is "the cunning agent of the king." The resemblances that he points out are noticeable, but they are only superficial ones and many differences are also there. To take but one example, Oberon is not trying to get away with an adulterous love-affair.

Next, taking up the Titania-Bottom affair Staton refers to *Venus and Adonis* because in it also an immortal female courts a mortal man. He points out seven points of similarity between *Venus and Adonis* and this love-affair.

The fourth view is given by Noel Purdon who equates Titania with Diana and Puck with Cupid. As a matter of fact he calls the play a "mythological Psychomachia" and draws many parallels between the play and classical myths. It is a complex and very learned discussion. He takes the fairies very seriously and draws parallels between them and the sylphs in Pope's *The Rape of the Lock* and the Lilliputs in Swift's *Gulliver's Travels*. The fairies are delightful creatures and therefore literary critics have not taken them seriously:

> None of Shakespeare's plays has suffered so constantly as this one from same kind of attention as a work of art that they give the others.[7]

He goes against the common idea that the spirits have been conceived in a vague and haphazard manner. Nor are they as native to England as is commonly supposed. Titania is another version of Diana, Puck is the counterpart of Cupid. The other fairies are the servitors of Diana. According to him this was a well-known Elizabethan concept. He quotes Nashe to support his argument:

> The Robin-good-fellows, Elfes, Fairies, Hobgoblins of our later age, which idolatrous former daies and the, fantasticall world of Greece ycleaped Fawnes, Satyres, Dryades and Hamadryades.[8]

These are the different views about the fairies in the *Dream* and most of them are modern. Earlier also literary critics had spent some thought on them, but not much analysis had been done. As the fairies are supernatural beings Aristotle's rules about them would naturally come to the mind of the earlier scholars. Aristotle had allowed the element of the supernatural in drama and Dryden had echoed this:

> ... poets may be allowed the liberty for describing things which really exist not, if they are founded on popular belief. Of this nature are fairies, pigmies and the extra-ordinary effects of magic... and thus are Shakespeare's *Tempest,* his *Midsummer Night's Dream* to be defended.[9]

Dr. Johnson, a hard-headed person, had also excused the fairies on the ground of tradition. He referred to Spenser in this connection, thus giving Shakespeare a great predecessor.

After this, in the twentieth century much work was done in this field. Frank Sidgwick lists the main characteristics of Shakespeare's fairies:

(a) They are usually the subjects of a king and queen.

(b) They are small in size, very light and swift.

(c) They are an integral part of nature.

(d) They like singing and dancing.

(e) They are invisible to humans.

(f) They prefer night to day.

(g) They interact with humans.[10]

These and many other traits have been pointed out by scholars. One of these traits is special to Shakespeare's fairies. He depicts them as benevolent, contrary to traditional popular belief:

> For the first time the fairies themselves are made consistently good. No longer do they function as the mischievous and dangerous beings they were believed to be.[11]

This is the case not only with the *Dream* but with *The Tempest* also. Bottom's case is a significant example of this benevolence. He is brought into fairy land but does not feel any ill effects. He comes back to his own world and there is no difference in time. He comes back with everyone else and at the same time. Many fairy tales tell us of men being taken to fairy land and coming back after the lapse of many years but no such thing happens here. Very often such men are restored to the world in a half-idiotic or insane condition, but Bottom is safe.

The fairies of the *Dream,* moreover, are no idle creatures. They are hard-working and are always busy. They are accomplished courtiers as well. Examples for all the traits mentioned so far can be found in the play. All these features make it seem that Shakespeare has changed the very nature of the traditional English fairy. Schanzer complains that he:

> ... has robbed it of its fearfulness and hence its reality, and turned it into a trifle light as air, the mere plaything of the imagination.[12]

Shakespeare has done this to suit the nature of the play. The *Dream* is a light-hearted romantic comedy and any being that inspired fear or even unease would have been out of place in it.

The name of Oberon, it is agreed, is taken from the French romance *Huon of Bordeaux* where the name Auberon can be found. Spenser also uses it. He is shown in this play as a king with great power over nature and magnanimous to humans. He sees Demetrius spurning Helena and has pity on her. When he sees how Puck has made a mess with the juice he rebukes Puck and tells him to put things right as soon as possible:

> This is thy negligence. Still thou mistak'st
> Or else commit'st thy knaveries wilfully.[13]

Not only does he undo all the mischief but at the end he, with his fairy court comes and blesses the wedded couples.

The only instance of mischief as far as he is concerned occurs when he causes Titania to fall in love with Bottom. In this entire incident he shows himself as a selfish husband. Moreover, he is conscious of the fact that their quarrel has brought about disorder in nature. But he cleverly shifts the blame on to Titania:

> Do you amend it then: it lies in you
> Why should Titania cross her Oberon?[14]

To a certain extent this is true. Both of them are being selfish and obstinate. So he uses the love-juice on her, but is careful to disenchant her as soon as his purpose is served. After all, this temporary tiff between husband and wife does not affect the human beings at all. As far the humans are concerned, he is totally benevolent. He brings happiness into the life of the Athenian lovers and showers blessings, though unsought.

Titania, like Oberon, shows herself to be obstinate over the changeling whom Oberon wants, but this refusal to give him up is the outcome of her love for the boy's dead mother who was her priestess as well as her friend:

> And for her sake do I rear up the boy
> And for her sake I will not part with him.[15]

She does not take any part in the affairs of the humans. She is made to fall in love with Bottom, but on being disenchanted is reconciled to Oberon. Her love for Bottom,however artificial, has made Frank Kermode give a very serious interpretation of Bottom's character, as has already been explained (*vide* Ch. 7, Bottom's Character, *supra*).

Puck the mischievous spirit is the fore-runner of Ariel in *The Tempest*. He, moreover, is a spirit well-known in England folklore, and is also known under the name of Robin Goodfellow. Puck is actually he generic name for a mischievous spirit. In this play, Shakespeare has shown him as an obedient servant who helps Oberon to bring about the union of the lovers. It is rue that he creates dissension between Lysander and Demetrius and also between Lysander and Hermia by mistaking the former for Demetrius. This is not done deliberately. It is an honest mistake. The only sign of mischief he shows is by putting the ass-head on Bottom. He, also, unravels the tangle he has made quite willingly and unites the lovers.

It is significant that it is he who has the honour of delivering the epilogue, thereby providing literary critics with food for thought about the theme:

> And this weak and idle theme
> No more yielding but a dream.[16]

His constant interaction with the world of humans has given him a semi-human aura. As C. Watts has, in this connection, observed:

> He becomes a hybrid entity, part fantasy and part substance, rather as Bottom was a mixture of ass and man.[17]

(B) THE MINOR CHARACTERS

There are but only a few dramatists who pay as much attention to their minor characters as Shakespeare did. It is one of the many reasons for his supremacy over his contemporaries. Even though a character comes on the stage for a very short time and speaks very little, he depicts him or her in such a way as to give individuality. The play under discussion is an early play, yet he has tried to individualise the minor characters here also.

(i) Hippolyta

Hippolyta is the first of the minor courtly characters to come on the stage. She is not only the queen of the Amazons, but is also on the verge of becoming Theseus's wife, thus becoming the queen of Athens as well. As such she should be treated as a major character, but her role in the play is so slight that one is forced to treat her as a minor one. She takes no part at all in the action. In fact there is no other character who is as expendable from the point of view of the action as she is. The only way in which she serves an important function is by consolidating the theme of love, providing an example of ideal married love with Theseus. She is the stabilizing influence on Theseus which makes him settle down after his adventurous life to become a good king, even an ideal one.

Like Theseus, she too is a character out of classical myths, but Shakespeare has altered her in several significant ways. It has for example, been said that Shakespeare intended her as well as Theseus for comic figures. The German critic Oechelhauser is of the opinion that whereas both Theseus and Hippolyta differ from their classical personalities, in Hippolyta's case the difference is more pronounced than it is with Theseus. Titania, jealous of Oberon's attraction for Hippolyta, refers to her in a slighting and contemptuous manner as a "bouncing Amazon", stressing her lack of feminine graces. Then he points out that both she and Theseus are comic figures, for they are both too old to appear as romantic lovers, particularly as truly young lovers are already present here:

> The roles of Theseus and Hippolyta acquire the genuine and befitting shade of comicality, when they are presented as a stout middle-aged pair of lovers, past their maturity.[18]

This is not a view with which other critics agree. Almost everyone thinks that she, together with Theseus, represents a sane and mature, stable and domestic love. The question of their age simply does not arise. They have an ageless, symbolic dimension.

From the classical point of view, she is the queen of the Amazons who were warrior females. They had abjured the society of men and used to kill all male children born to them. They were looked upon as a class of women who had overturned the accepted social order and disturbed the hierarchy. Symbolically, they represent a serious offence in society:

> Specifically they had come to signify a false usurpation of the duties of the male reason by the lower female passions.[19]

This is the mediaeval attitude carried on into the Renaissance and Shakespeare in making his hero marry her was presenting a spectacle that was not acceptable from the classical point of view, but eminently reasonable from an Elizabethan one. It shows Theseus, representing Order and Rationality, governing misrule and unreason.

She, like Theseus, appears only thrice in the play, once in the first scene of Act I, then in the last part of the first scene of Act IV, and finally in the last Act. She speaks only once in each of the first two appearances. In the last scene she says that she does not want to see the playlet being put up by the mechanicals. When however, she is overruled by her husband she makes the best of a bad job and enters into the spirit of the thing, showing that she is enjoying the show. Even in these short speeches our poet has been able to individualize her. One such touch , in particular, has been pointed out by Noel Purdon. He refers to the hunting-scene described by Hippolyta in her second appearance. She is describing the hunts in which she had taken part:

> I was with Hercules and Cadmus once,
> When in a wood of Crete they bayed the bear
> With hounds of Sparta: Never did I hear
> Such gallant chiding; for—besides the groves—

> The skies, the fountains, every region near,
> Seemed all one mutual cry. I never heard
> So musical a discord, such sweet thunder.[20]

This description tells us that she too is a great huntress. Greek mythology does not have many female characters among mortals who have prowess as sports-women. Besides the Amazons, who are known better for their warlike valour than as sports-women, there is only one, the princess Atlanta. Hippolyta invites comparison with her as well as with the divine huntress Diana. This highly individualizing touch is entirely of Shakespeare's creation:

> ... he is careful to make Hippolyta as well a huntress of heroic stature, like Atalanta or Diana. This he does by the invention of a mythological scene which she can refer to.[21]

(ii) Egeus

Egeus is the second of the minor courtly characters to enter the stage. As such he is the stock example of the heavy and angry father who is a domestic tyrant and wants to keep everyone under his thumb. He does not give any reasons for preferring Demetrius to Lysander and wants to marry Hermia off to the former by any means he can. He is ready even to threaten her with death, which the ancient law of Athens has made it possible for him to do:

> I beg the ancient privilege of Athens:
> As she is mine, I may dispose of her:
> Which shall be either to this gentleman
> Or to her death; according to our law
> Immediately provided in that case.[22]

After this he speaks only once in this scene, to affirm his preference for Demetrius, and we see him next when, in Act IV, sc. i Theseus enters the wood with his retinue. It is he who identifies the lovers lying asleep on the ground and when Lysander is explaining the facts about their elopement, he interrupts him to insist once more upon his rights:

> Enough, enough, my lord: you have enough.
> I beg the law, the law upon his head—[23]

It is seen that he does not speak at all after this, not even when Theseus clearly says that he will go against his wishes, and get Lysander and Hermia, and Demetrius and Helena married that very day. He is the only character who is not present on the stage in the last scene. He is an example of how economical Shakespeare's dramatic technique is. He needed this character to bring about the kind of situation which will bring the lovers to the wood. As soon as the character has served his purpose he is discarded. A stock character, he presents patriarchy at its worst.

(iii) Philostrate

This is the last character to come on the stage. He comes in the last scene, and there is a valid reason for his lateness in appearing. He is Theseus's Master of Revels, i.e., the official who is in charge of court entertainments. Thus he has to provide some entertainment after the marriage of Theseus and Hippolyta, and it is him Theseus calls to find out about the shows that are going to be presented. He gives Theseus a list to choose from and when Theseus chooses Bottom's play, tries to dissuade him, for the show is sub-standard:

> No, my noble lord,
> It is not for you. I have heard it over
> And it is nothing, nothing in the world.[24]

But Theseus overrules him and after this he hardly speaks. His is an entirely functional role and he speaks very little, but Shakespeare has developed his character significantly within even this small, compass. He is seen to be a conscientious official, one who is no shirker, but performs his duties efficiently. He has seen all the items to be presented and is able to judge their quality. He also keeps in mind the suitability of the play to the occasion, for one of the objections he raises about the show is that it is a tragedy and therefore unsuitable for a marriage celebration.

(iv) The Mechanicals

There are six of these in the play and though Bottom is unquestionably the leader and a major character, Quince is the director of the playlet. All of them make their appearance together in Act I, sc. ii. It is Quince's house that is the venue and they have all gathered together to decide about rehearsing their play. Quince has the script and it is he who assigns the roles to the actors. All the characters have been given names that are indicative of their trade. The name Quince obliquely refers to "quines" or "quoins" which are wedges made of wood used in carpentry, and Quince is a carpenter by trade.

He shows himself to be a considerate and accommodating person. When Bottom suggests a prologue he readily agrees to it. He is a sensible man and knows where to draw the line in accepting the suggestions put forward by the others, as for example when Bottom wants to play the Lion. After distributing the script to each actor he fixes the time and place for the next meeting.

In the forest he leads and directs the rehearsals, incorporating all relevant suggestions. When Bottom enters with the ass-head it is he who, in a typical malapropism, exclaims a sentence that has since become famous:

> Bless thee, Bottom, bless thee ! Thou art translated.[25]

In Act IV, sc. ii., which is the shortest scene of the play it is he who eulogises Bottom:

> You have not in all Athens a man able to discharge Pyramus but he.... Yea, and the best person too; and he is a very paramour for a sweet voice.[26]

After this, when the play is being staged, it is he who delivers a wonderful prologue in which Shakespeare, by merely misplacing the punctuation marks has created humour in a masterly fashion thus:

> If we offend, it is with our good will.
> That you should think, we come not to offend
> But with good will.[27]

After a few more of these jumbled lines, however, he recovers himself and delivers the rest of the long Prologue quite sensibly, introducing the characters and telling the story. Like all the other mechanicals except Bottom, he is present in these four scenes and the dramatist has individualized him quite sharply. In comparison with him the others are seen to be vague portrayals.

The other mechanicals are also named according to their trade. Thus Snug the joiner is a man whose trade is to fit joints snugly. Flute is a bellows mender—an artisan who often had to mend church organs. Besides, his voice might have been a fluty voice and this makes Quince give him a female role. Snout the tinker's name suggests "spout" and spouts belong to kettles which are mended by tinkers. Starveling is a tailor and tailors are always supposed to be half-starved thin persons.

All these characters like Quince, appear in four scenes and speak a few lines. They have not been sharply individualized and literary critics always mention them (except for Bottom) in a group. All these mechanicals serve the important purpose of providing a comic dimension to the play, as well as enlarging its scope by bringing in the working class. The name "mechanicals" has been bestowed upon them by Puck:

> A crew of patches, rude mechanicals
> That work for bread upon Athenian stalls.[28]

A valid objection that had been raised quite early is that this group of characters is made up of Englishmen and are out of place in ancient Athens. There is, however, nothing so typically English in them as to mark them out. The trades they follow are such as had existed long ago and still exist. They have English names, but they can exist anywhere at any time.

REFERENCES

1. Dr. Johnson, *op. cit.*, p. 30.
2. Price, A., *op. cit.*, p. 34.
3. *Ibid.*, p. 142.
4. Hunter, G.K., *Contrasts Rather than Interactions in Price*, A., *op. cit.*, p. 122.
5. Act III, sc. ii. ll. 461-64, p. 73.
6. Schanzer, E., *The Moon and the Fairies* in Price, A., *op. cit.*, pp. 71-72.
7. Purdon, Noel, *The Mythological Psychomachia* in Price A., *op. cit.*, p. 171.
8. *Ibid.*, p. 172.
9. *Ibid.*, p. 26.

10. Purdon, Noel, *The Mythological Psychomachia* in Price A., *op. cit.*, p. 47.
11. *Ibid.*, p. 59.
12. Schanzer, E., *op. cit.*, p. 72
13. Act III, sc. ii., ll. 345-46, p. 70.
14. Act II, sc. i., ll. 118-19, p. 46.
15. Act II, sc. i., ll. 136-37, p. 46.
16. Act V, sc. i., ll. 412-13, p. 93.
17. Watts, C. *op. cit.*, p. 16.
18. Oechelhauser, W., *op. cit.*, pp. 40-41.
19. Olson, Paul, *op. cit.*, p. 79.
20. Act IV. sc. i., ll. 111-117, p. 77.
21. Purdon, Noel, *op. cit.*, p. 179.
22. Act I, sc. i., ll. 41-45, p. 34.
23. Act IV. sc. ii., ll. 153-54, p. 78.
24. Act V, sc. i., ll. 76-78, p. 84.
25. Act III, sc. i., line 108, p. 58.
26. Act IV, sc. ii., ll. 5-10, p. 80.
27. Act V, sc. i., ll. 108-10, p. 85.
28. Act III, sc. ii., ll. 9-10, p. 61.

9

The Plot-Structure

Aristotle had declared the plot to be the soul of tragedy and the same can be said about comedy as well. They basic difference between the two, of course is that while tragedies have an unhappy ending, it is the opposite with comedies. The comedies, also, have a more complex structure for they have more intrigues and episodes. Tragedies are more streamlined. There are many rules concerning structure that have been laid down by Aristotle and his followers. Some of these rules shall be mentioned now. It has to be remembered that the rules refer to tragedy, for Aristotle had not written about comedy. Most of them however, can be applied to comedies as well.

(A) CLASSICAL RULES AND THE DREAM

The Rules of the Unities: The so-called rules of the three unities—unity of action, unity of time and unity of place—generally attributed to Aristotle came to England mainly through the writings of the Italian Renaissance: Scaliger, Minturno, Castelvetro *et al.* Aristotle speaks mainly of the unity of action and only incidentally about the unity of time. He does not say anything at all about the unity of place. It was due to the misreading of Aristotle by the Italian writers that the unity of place was also regarded as one of the Aristotelian unities. However, these rules have become famous as the Three Unities. These are: (a) the Unity of Action, (b) the Unity of Time and (c) the Unity of Place. It is a well-known fact that Shakespeare did not take these rules very seriously, except for in *The Tempest* which from this point of view is a very "regular" play. The *Dream* does not contain flagrant violation of the rules but nor does it observe them. Shakespeare's attitude is one of sovereign indifference.

(a) The Unity of Action. This rule declares that there should be no mingling of serious and trivial incidents. This is specially important for tragedies, but is relevant for comedies as well. Just as a tragedy should not have comic actions in it, so a comedy, too, should not have tragic actions in it. Pity and terror which are the emotions produced by tragic actions have been assigned to tragedies. Comedies should have actions that produce laughter. Though this rule is more relevant for satirical comedies yet it can be applied to romantic comedies like the play *The Dream*.

We often come across serious actions in Shakespeare's comedies, along with comic ones. There is, however, no impression of anomaly, for the serious actions do not produce pity and terror, except in the case of Shylock in *The Merchant of Venice*. In the play under discussion tragedy threatens Hermia, but it is avoided. Again, the action in the playlet is basically tragic and would have clashed with the mood of the play, but the poet's artistry invests it with comic aura and divests it of tragic potentialities.

(b) The Unity of Time. Ideally, the time covered by the story of the play should be of the same length as covered by the actual performance on the stage. If the performance takes two hours, then so should the action. This seems to be impossible, but it had been achieved by the classical dramatists. Aristotle had set the limit at "a single revolution of the sun." The story of a play should take, at the most about a full day. This also is difficult, but it has been done, notably by Ben Jonson and by Shakespeare himself in *The Tempest.*

Shakespeare does not usually care much about the rules and *The Tempest* is an exception. In many of his plays it is not possible to observe this rule, as for example the chronicle plays. The most notorious violation of the unity of time occurs in *The Winter's Tale* in which sixteen years are covered.

The present play presents a curious case. According to the internal evidence (i.e. the time mentioned within the play by the characters) four days have been covered, yet when the actual performance takes place, or in the case of reading when the scene by scene progress is calculated, it will seem that two days and two nights have been covered. Theseus, in the very opening speech tells us:

> Now fair Hippolyta, our nuptial hour
> Draws on apace four happy days bring in
> Another moon.[1]

In the last scene the wedding has taken place. Thus, the time covered would seem to take four days and four nights. But practically the time-scheme is different. In the first scene Lysander and Hermia decide to meet in the forest the next night. Lysander says:

> If thou lov'est me, then,
> Steal forth thy father's house tomorrow night:

and Hermia with many vows, agrees:

> In that same place thou hast appointed me,
> Tomorrow truly will I meet with thee.[2]

The mechanicals also decide to meet in the forest the same night. Then the main action takes place in the forest the next night, which dawns at the end of Act IV, sc. ii. Act V takes place later the same day beginning in the evening at ending possibly at midnight. Thus the action takes two nights and two days and part of the third night. There is, thus, some confusion concerning the actual time covered by the play.

(c) **The Unity of Place.** According to this rule, there should be no changes of scenes in a play. The action should take place in one place only. This is almost impossible though the classical dramatists had managed to do it. Ben Jonson also had observed the rule though he gives a few changes of scenes.

Shakespeare did not observe this rule either. His scenes, like those of Jonson, range within the same city, but even more frequently, change over different kingdoms. This had been condemned by the neo-classical critics of his own time as well as those of later ages. It should be remembered that Dr. Johnson, one of the greatest neo-classical critics, had defended his violation of these rules.

So far as the present play is concerned, there are a few changes of scenes, though actually there are only three such changes. The first and the last scenes take place in Theseus's palace. The second scene and the penultimate one take place in Quince's house and all the scenes between them take place in the forest. The different scene-changes are very systematically balanced.

These and quite a few other such rules about plot were given by Aristotle. His works were not available to the Elizabethans, but those of his followers and commentators were. One of these was Donatus, who had not only explained Aristotle, but had added some ideas of his own. The scheme of the plot he had given had become known to all Elizabethan writers. The first section of the play (as indeed, Aristotle also declares) is the Prologue. This, usually, is a short speech coming before the actual action begins. It tells the reader about the theme and the story of the ensuing play. Usually the Elizabethan dramatists incorporated the prologue within the first scene of the play in order to introduce the play. The first section of the first scene of the *Dream,* till Egeus and the other come, is the prologue of this play.

Besides these, there are certain other rules for drama that were practised by the Elizabethans in tragedy as well as in comedy. "Peripeteia" or the Reversal of fortune is such a device. This strategy is usually employed in a tragedy and as such has a negative sense because it implies the fall of the hero from a high to a low status. When used with reference to comedy however it has a positive sense for it then can mean a change from adversity to prosperity or from misery to bliss. Hermia, in the beginning of the play, is on the point of losing her life. Escaping from this dire fate, she comes to the forest where there is more misery in store for her, as Lysander forsakes her for Helena. After this however, things improve and at the end of the play she is united to Lysander.

Very often, specially in comedies, the plot becomes so intricate that it becomes difficult to bring about a happy ending. In such cases there is the classical strategy of the *deus ex machina.* In the classical plays a god, like Apollo, Zeus or someone else would come on the stage and, with his divine powers, smooth out all the difficulties so that a happy ending can be brought about. In English plays this function is given over to some person in authority, like the king, the duke, etc. Aristotle is not in favour of this device, but it is widely used by dramatists. In our play it is mainly Oberon who carries out the function of the *deus ex machina*. He makes Demetrius fall in love with Helena so that the way to two weddings become clear. Again, towards the end, Theseus acts as a *deus* by overruling Egeus:

> Egeus, I will overbear your will;
> For in the temple, by and, by, with us,
> These couples shall eternally be knit.[3]

Thus an immortal and a mortal being are in turn given the function of a *deus ex machnia*.

(B) CERTAIN ELIZABETHAN FEATURES IN THE DREAM

In the Old Classical Comedies there is but one plot only, and Aristotle was not in favour of more than one plot in a play. As the New Classical Comedy developed, changes crept in and very often there are two plots in the plays of Plautus and Terence. The Elizabethans developed their own plays on the model of these writers. Ben Jonson, who followed Terence, made all his plays at least double-plotted if not multiple-plotted. True to this Elizabethan feature, Shakespeare's plays also have more than one plot. Usually, as in all these plays, there is one main plot and one or more subplots. These latter usually involve humble (as opposed in noble) characters, and are comic ones, provoking laughter. *A Midsummer Night's Dream* is a play with three plots—the main plot concerned with the Athenians, the fairy plot with supernatural characters, and the comic plot with the mechanicals.

In the main plot we have the Athenian nobles, and the main interest is love. Lysander and Hermia love each other, but as Egeus, the father, is opposed to their union they are forced to elope, for an ancient law decrees that a father can put a disobedient daughter to death. While crossing a forest during the night they are observed by the fairies in the forest. Their case is complicated by another pair of young Athenians, Demetrius and Helena, of whom Demetrius loves Hermia and is in his turn loved by Helena. In the forest, finally the tangle is unravelled by supernatural intervention so that Lysander-Hermia make one couple of lovers and Demetrius-Helena is another couple. In the morning they are found in the forest by Duke Theseus, the ruler of Athens, who has come out to hunt. The same day the two couples are married along with the royal couple, Theseus and Hippolyta.

The second plot, which nearly equals the main one in importance, involves the fairies in the forest. Titania the fairy queen has a human child in her train whom Oberon the king wants in his own retinue. He drips the magic juice of a flower which makes her fall in love with the ass-headed Bottom. This makes her so ashamed of herself that she gives up the boy to Oberon. When Oberon gets the boy he disenchants her from her enslavements of unnatural love and the King and Queen are united. Incidentally Oberon, who is full of goodwill towards humans, makes Demetrius fall in love with Helena. Here some difficulty is introduced by way of intrigue, for Puck the chief attendant of Oberon, makes a mistake and at first makes Lysander fall in love with Helena. All this is later smoothed out.

The third plot concerns six artisans of Athens who want to prepare a show for the entertainment of Theseus and Hippolyta, who are shortly to be married. They go to the forest to rehearse the play. Here Puck puts the head of an ass on Bottom the weaver and this is the character with whom Titania is made to fall in love. He is relieved of his ass-head when Titania is disenchanted and the play they had prepared is duly put up to amuse the courtiers at the end of the play.

This playlet that the mechanicals perform is again a typically Elizabethan feature. Such playlets occur again and again in these plays, as in Kyd's *The Spanish Tragedy* and Shakespeare's own *Hamlet.* The playlet *Pyramus and Thisby* is, in addition, a play celebrating the three weddings, so it takes the place of a masque.

After this brief account of the typically Elizabethan features in our play, let us turn our attention to the sources from which the poet took his plot.

(C) THE SOURCES OF THE DREAM

Elizabethan drama based its plots on many other sources, like histories, romances, stories, etc. It was very rare for a play to have been created entirely out of the writer's imagination. All the writers took help from pre-existing sources and so did Shakespeare. Such gathering together of material from various sources gave proof of the dramatist's organizing capacity and dramatic insight. Very extensive studies have been made of the sources from which Shakespeare took the material of his plays and Geoffrey Bullough has given no less than eleven sources of the *Dream*.

It is a well-known fact that this play had been produced for an aristocratic wedding, though it is not known for sure which wedding it was. Bullough has remarked:

> In keeping with the hymeneal occasion Shakespeare treated the play as a marry prank, exercising great ingenuity to unify a hotch-potch of materials.[4]

He gives no less than eleven sources under the heading *Probable Sources*. These are:

I *The Knight's Tale,* in Chaucer's *The Canterbury Tales.*

II *The Life of Theseus,* in Plutarch's *Lives,* translated by Lord North.

III *Huon of Bordeaux* translated by Lord Berniers.

IV *The Discovery of Witchcraft* by Reginald Scot.

V *Thesaurus Lingua Romance et Britannicae* Thomas Cooper.

VI *The Golden Ass* by Apuleius.

VII *Discovery of the Witches*—a different Book and Chapter of the same work as under IV.

VIII *Thesaurus Linguae Latinae of Britannicae* by Thomas Cooper.

IX *Metamorphoses* by Ovid, translated by Arthur Golding.

X *A Handfull of Pleasant Delites* by Clement Robert and others.

XI *The Tragedy of Pyramus and Thisbe.*

The first of these, *The Knight's Tale,* is the first tale in *Canterbury Tales.* The story of Theseus and Hippolyta has been told here. It mentions how Theseus conquered the Amazons and married their queen and brought her to Athens:

He conquered al the regne of Femenye,
That whilom was y-cleped Saithia;
And wedded the queene Ypolita,
And broughte hire hoom with hym in his countree.[5]

Theseus is depicted here as a great and noble duke and this is how Shakespeare, too, presents him.

The second probable source is the *Life of Theseus* from Plutarch. He too presents Theseus as a man of enterprise, with great organizing capacities, so he could bring all the men of Attica under his rule. Plutarch tells the entire story of his life, offering critical comments all the time. He also mentions that some historians say that he married Hippolyta though Plutarch himself does not give this story much importance. He later compares Theseus with Romulus and finds the former to be guilty of indulging excessively in too many irresponsible love-affairs.

The third probable source is the mediaeval romance of Huon of Bordeaux. Shakespeare had taken the concept of the fairy king from here:

> In that wood abideth a King of the Fayryes named Oberon; he is of height but of three foote.[6]

Oberon shows himself to the knights and helps them, as he helps the benighted humans in this play.

The fourth source is Reginald Scot's famous book and Bullough has given it twice, for two different kinds of material. In the first place he quotes from Bk. IV, Chap, X; B. Bk. VII, Chap, II, and XV. All of these three chapters tell us of Robin

Goodfellow, how housewives would put out white bread and milk for him at night. The fairy to whom Puck talks in Act II, sc. i, explains his nature in detail:

> You are that shrewd and knavish sprite
> Called Robin Godfellow. Are you not he
> That frights the maidens of the villagery
> Skim milk, and sometimes labour in the queen.[7]

The fifth source is named an *Analogue*. This is Thomas Cooper's *Thesaurus* (the full name is given above). It tells the story of King Midas who had been given ass's ears by Apollo. It is thought that Shakespeare got the idea of putting an ass-head on Bottom from this.

The sixth source however is a more likely one for Bottom's ass-head. This is the famous work. *The Golden Ass,* by Apuleius (*vide* Ch. 7, Bottom's Character, *supra*). Lucius the narrator is turned into an ass in this work. Shakespeare however, steers the middle course between King Midas and Apuleius, for he gives Bottom the head of an ass, not just two ears, and not the entire body of an ass either.

The seventh source given by Bullough is the same book by Scot that he gives for the source of Puck. Here he gives Bk. V, Chap. III and Bk. XIII Chap. XIX which tell us about men being transformed into asses and how they could be transformed back again.

The eighth analogue is another *Thesaurus* by Thomas Cooper, which tells the story of Pyramus and Thisbe and Shakespeare gives it in the playlet. The same story is given by Ovid, which Bullough cites as the ninth source. This tale is in verse whereas Cooper gives it in prose. The story is found in the tenth source also which also, like Ovid's is a narrative poem. The eleventh and last source is a verse play that dramatizes the same story. The languages used in this last one is ornate and artificial, the kind of language that Shakespeare makes fun of in his own version.

It can thus be seen that Shakespeare takes his material from many different sources and then blends them into a superb and harmonious whole, rejecting superfluous material and making other adjustments wherever necessary. This choosing and welding together shows great organizing capacity and this can be seen in each play of Shakespeare.

(D) THE PLOT OF THE DREAM

The *Dream* has three plots, which Shakespeare has welded together to create a unified whole. There are not many plays with three plots in them, specially three plots with such widely divergent characters in them. As has been pointed out above, the story has been derived from many sources, and shows his individual and original talent for bringing together the element of romance (which the contemporary audience wanted) and those of farcical comedy. All these are mixed with the supernatural element that was so dear to the heart of the Elizabethans. No small craftsmanship was needed.

It has to be noted that though the royal couple Theseus and Hippolyta take part in the play they are not the main characters Theseus, however important he might be in Athenian society, is not the hero of the play. It is the Athenian lovers who form the nucleus of the play and it is this plot which should be designated as the main one. A notable fact is that the main plot gives, not the eternal triangle, but a more complex situation. Lysander and Hermia love each other, but the bride's father favours another suitor, Demetrius. Thus there is already a triangle here. A fourth character provides intrigue in the main plot. It is Helena who is in love with Demetrius. Thus we have two intersecting love-triangles here: Lysander-Hermia-Demetrius and Demetrius-Helena-Hermia. More complications in these relationships are introduced by the fairy sub-plot.

In the fairy sub-plot we have the King and the Queen who are at outs with each other. It would seem that this is a completely independent plot. Our poet, however, links them together. First of all he brings the four Athenians to the forest where the fairies dwell. Then Oberon, seeing Helena suffering the pangs of unrequited love, directs Puck to put the love-juice on Demetrius's eyes but Puck, by mistake, puts it into Lysander's. Thus the two plots are linked together. Then again to counteract this mischance, Oberon puts the juice on Demetrius's eyelids and another link is established. So now the relationship of the main-plot characters stand thus: Lysander and Demetrius both love Helena whereas Helena loves Demetrius and Hermia loves Lysander. Once more, while all four are asleep, the love-juice is put on Lysander's eyes and so for the third time the main and the fairy sub-plot are brought together. All tangles are unravelled by supernatural agency.

The mechanicals' sub-plot is linked to the main one because they are putting up a play to celebrate Theseus's wedding. They come to the forest to rehearse and here Puck puts the ass-head on Bottom so this plot also becomes linked to the fairy plot. Then Titania falls in love with him and a second link is forged between the two.

In the last scene all three plots are brought together in a masterly manner. The mechanicals perform their play to celebrate the triple wedding and the fairies come to bless the married couples.

It would seem almost impossible to put so many events and different characters harmoniously in one play. Shakespeare, however, alternates his scenes with great artistry between the main and the two sub-plots. A scene-by-scene synopsis will show how the interweaving has been carried out:

Act I, sc. i — Located at Theseus's palace in Athens. The main plot characters meet.

Act I, sc ii — Located at Quince's house in Athens. The mechanicals meet.

Act II, sc. i — Located in the forest. The fairy plot characters meet. Demetrius and Helena enter. Oberon directs Puck to put the juice on Demetrius's eyes.

Act II, sc. ii — The forest. Oberon puts the juice on Titania's eyes. Lysander and Hermia enter and sleep. Lysander is made to fall in love with Helena.

Act III, sc. i — The forest. The mechanicals come in to rehearse. Puck puts the ass-head on Bottom and Titania falls in love with him.

Act III, sc. ii — The forest. Oberon puts the juice on Demetrius's eyes. The four lovers quarrel, then fall asleep. Puck drips the juice on Lysander's eyelids.

Act IV, sc. i — The forest. Oberon disenchants Titania. Bottom is relieved of his ass-head. Theseus enters. Sleeping lovers awakened. Triple marriage decided.

Act IV, sc. ii — Quince's house in Athens. Bottom comes back. Preparations for staging the playlet.

Act V — Only one scene. Located at Theseus's palace. All the characters assemble. Playlet staged. Fairies come to dance and bless the couples. The Epilogue is spoken by Puck.

It can be seen from this scheme how very carefully Shakespeare has alternated the scenes among the different plots, often dividing a scene into distinct parts in order to deal separately with separate plots (*vide* Ch. 5, *supra*). Then he starts interweaving them. Complications ensue. In Act IV sc. i. all three plots are brought together, and finally all tangles are unravelled. The plot presents a unified and harmonious whole G.K. Chesterton calls it "amazingly symmetrical" and declares:

> The supreme literary merit of *A Midsummer Night's Dream* is a merit of design.[8]

There are many learned discussions on the plot of this play. A three-movement pattern has been found in it by Paul A. Olson. He finds a highly philosophical pattern in it: it begins with the exposition of an established order, moves on to a Fall of this order and ends with the re-establishment of the harmony it began with. Thus in Act I we have:

> ... the movement towards an orderly subordination of the female and her passions to the more reasonable male.[9]

Then the second movement of the play begins with Act II and includes Act III. Here we have the breakdown of order and harmony and most appropriately, argues the critic, it takes place in a forest which stands here for the lack of order and reason:

> In a more generalized sense, the dark wood could signify the confusions which beset the earthly life.[10]

With Act IV and the disenchantment of Titania the third movement of the play begins. Here we have the gradual restoration of order and sanity.

John Dover Wilson finds four plots in the play instead of three, for he takes the marriage of Theseus and Hippolyta as another plot. He is full of praise for the manner in which the dramatist has managed all these four plots and compares him with Ben Jonson. He points out a crucial difference between these two:

> While Ben Jonson's plots work towards the confounding or exposing of his characters Shakespeare's find their consummation in happiness.[11]

This aspect of the plots, however, is nothing extraordinary, since Ben Jonson's comedies are satirical comedies and the *Dream* is a romantic one.

Many other interpretations of the plot are there but all the critics agree that it is a masterpiece of stage craft and strategies in which a medley of disparate elements have been brought together to create a unified whole. We shall now cast a look at the inset play, or the play-within-the-play, *Pyramus and Thisbe.*

As has been pointed out earlier, this was a well-known Elizabethan feature, popularized by Kyd in his *The Spanish Tragedy*. It offered the dramatist a welcome chance for introducing variety and entertainment. The device served many purposes, that have been summed up very succinctly by Fluchère. According to him it:

> ... was introduced into the play to underline its moral significance, to comment on the theme, or to help solve the plot. It added the spectacular element of the unfamiliar, the chance of music and of sumptuous costumes, the entertainment of the dance and of the piquancy of parody.[12]

This playlet is definitely a parody and as far as the theme is concerned, it adds a new dimension to the theme of love, for it gives tragic love, which is at the same time, ridiculous. Only Shakespeare's genius could have produced an unparallelled work like this.

As has been mentioned above, he had no less than three sources for his story, two of which were narrative poems and the third a play. They are written in highly rhetorical language, particularly the play, and Shakespeare took great delight in parodying this bombastic language. Quince the director is also perhaps the script-writer. The story is one of tragic love and it is quite clear that none of them knows the difference between a tragedy and a comedy. They call the playlet a "most lamentable comedy." The actors had, in the rehearsal scene, decided how to present the play, making every provision for the supposed reactions of the noble audience. The play opens with a Prologue which is a masterly composition for Shakespeare has, by only changing the punctuation, produced comic effect:

> If we offend, it is with our good will.
> That you should think, we come not to offend
> But with good will. To show our simple skill,
> That is the true beginning of our end.[13]

Then, after the Prologue when the other characters have withdrawn, Snout comes in as the Wall and declares that he is not a wall in truth but a man named Snout. Thus in every instance parody and good-humoured mockery afford the courtly audience hilarious entertainment. Starveling comes in to show Moonshine. He carries a lantern in his hand to stand for the moon and he himself is the man in the moon with a bush in his other hand. Snug tells the audience that though he is representing a lion they need not be afraid, for he is actually only Snug the joiner.

The playlet tells the story of tragic love in which the hero and the heroine both die by their own hands. Yet Shakespeare presents it in such a way as to provide endless comic laughter. It must be remembered that it is performed to entertain newly-married couples and paradoxically, this is exactly what it does. It really is what it purports to be, "a most lamentable comedy," a merry and tragic play, providing comic laughter through the ineptitude of the actors.

There are many different ways in which its relationship to the main plot and its functions have been explained. Keeping in mind that it echoes the theme of love, E.K. Chambers says that it is:

> but a burlesque presentment of the same theme which has occupied us throughout.[14]

Later critics, like Frank Kermode, Paul Olson and others, repeat nearly the same idea from a different viewpoint. Thus, about fifty years later Noel Purdon says:

> Shakespeare, both in the events and language of *Pyramus and Thisbe* is parodying the play that he himself is writing. If we read the play-scene as his comment on his own efforts to provide a marriage-play it has double point.[15]

(E) THE SUPERNATURAL ELEMENT

Supernatural characters and events play a very important part in this play. The presence of such element, the element "the marvellous" was recognized and appreciated by Aristotle:

> The marvellous should be represented in tragedy.... The marvellous is a source of pleasure.[16]

Though this remark refers specially to tragedy, it is applicable to all plays. Aristotle had another remark to offer in this connection:

> Probable impossibilities are to be preferred to improbable possibilities.[17]

The element of the marvellous is present in our play from the beginning to the end. As a matter of fact it permeates the entire play. All the complications in the plot are brought about be them. They, indeed, make up a whole world in themselves—a fairy-land. yet this fairy-land is within the purview of the humans to such an extent that the fairies take a benevolent interest in the human characters, and bring about all the turns and twists of the plot. We have three levels of fairy characters in the play just as we have three levels of human characters—the royal ones, the aristocrat and the working class. All of them play their own parts and make the play a success to such an extent that the final impression left is that of the enchanted fairy-land and the humans recede into the background. A more extensive discussion of the fairy character is to be found on the foregoing chapter, Chapter 8.

REFERENCES

1. Act I, sc. i., ll. 1-3, p. 33.
2. Act I, sc. i., ll. 163-64 and 177-78, p. 37.
3. Act IV, sc. i., ll. 178-80, p. 79.
4. Bullough, G., *The Narrative and Dramatic Sources of Shakespeare,* Vol. I, London, Routledge and Kegan Paul, 1957, pp. 36-37.
5. *Ibid.*, p. 377.
6. *Ibid.*, p. 390.
7. Act II, sc. i., ll. 33-36, pp. 43-44.
8. Price, A., *op. cit.*, p. 43.
9. Olson, Paul, A., *The Meaning of Court Marriage,* in Price, A., *op. cit.*, p. 78.
10. *Ibid.*, p. 82.
11. Wilson, John Dover, *Shakespeare's Happy Comedies,* London, Faber Paper Covered ed., p. 186.
12. Fluchère, H., *op. cit.*, p. 127.
13. Act V, sc. i., ll. 108-11, p. 85.
14. Chambers, E.K., *Shakespeare: A Survey,* New York 1926, p. 87.
15. Purdon, N., *The Mythological Psychomachia* in Price, A., *op. cit.*, p. 181.
16. Dorsch, T.S., ed. & transl., *Classical Literary Criticism,* Penguin Books, 1975, p. 68.
17. *Ibid.*

10

Imagery and Symbolism

(A) IMAGERY

Some of the elements that make poetry effective by embellishing its diction are imagery and symbols. Modern critics have taken great pains to emphasize this aspect of our poet's works. The function of his imagery, the relationship between the theme of the play and its images, the development of his imagery—all these have been studied in meticulous detail. H. Fluchere has given a definition of imagery that is not only succint but comprehensive as well.

> Imagery may shortly be defined as a concrete illustration drawn upon by the poet to clarify or embellish the object that he seeks to describe.[1]

Shakespeare's images are more complex than this definition describes, for they do not merely clarify or embellish. They have certain other important functions as well.

It is often impossible to differentiate between rhetorical figures, images and symbols. These three are integrally related and there are frequent overlappings. An image, for example, is usually a figure of speech and, often enough, it is elevated to the level of a symbol as well. Fluchère has explained this with great insight:

> No strict rule allows us to say at what point we pass from the plane of pure rhetoric to the plane of pure psychology, and even the metaphysical plane, in the use of imagery.[2]

Moreover, according to the method of categorization, the same image will come under different kinds of categories. A sense image will also be a nature image or a domestic image or any other. This is a universal feature of all images.

The simplest of the images, and the easiest to understand, are sense-images. They are of five kinds, corresponding to the five human senses. Thus there are visual, auditory, olfactory, gustatory and tactile images, corresponding respectively to the eye, the ear, the nose, the tongue and the skin. Again there might often be a mixing and mingling of sense-images that is known as synaesthesia.

We shall now look at the images in only one scene of the play, the first scene of the first Act and try to analyse them. This will give the serious student an idea of the wealth of imagery in the entire play. Shakespeare's poetry is very rich in all kinds of sense-images. Hippolyta uses a vivid visual image in the very beginning of the play:

> And then the moon, like a silver bow
> New-bent in heaven, shall behold the night
> Of our solemnities.[3]

It has to be noted that this image of the moon, in itself a visual image, itself is portrayed as looking down on earth, and at the marriage. It thus, involves two different stages of a visual context (a) the characters looking up at the moon and (b) the moon looking down at the marriage. Apart from that it is an astronomical or, more specifically, a lunar image as well.

Egeus uses an auditory image in which he is accusing Lysander of having stolen Hermia's heart:

> Thou hast, by moonlight, at her window sung
> With feigning voice, verses of feigning love.[4]

A very dynamic visual image has been used by Lysander in describing love:

> Brief as the lightning in the collied night
> That (in a spleen) unfolds both heaven and earth,
> And ere a man hath power to say "Behold!"
> The jaws of darkness do devour it up.[5]

This passage uses both visual and auditory images, for the man seeing the lightning speaks the word "Behold." Along with this there is the image of the jaws of darkness which are devouring the light, i.e. a gustatory image is also here.

Next to visual images come the nature images. They are not only plentiful in this play, but it has been said that the *Dream* is superior to all other plays in this field. It can be compared with only two other parallels, *King Lear* and *The Tempest.* Even then, the *Dream* leaves the latter far behind:

> Compared to the nature-world of *A Midsummer Night's Dream,* however, the world of flora and fauna in *The Tempest* is less lovely, less Elizabethan, less poetical and aesthetic.[6]

A lovely nature-image is used by Theseus in the first scene to compare the married girl with an unmarried one:

> But earthlier happy is the rose distilled,
> Than that which, withering on the virgin thorn,
> Grows, lives and dies in single blessednes.[7]

This image, too, is not as simple as it looks, because here not one but two images are involved. One is that of the flower which blossoms on its stalk and is then used by man to make perfumes. The second is that of the one which withers on its stalk without being of any use to anyone. Again, there is the suggestion of an olfactory image in the word "distilled," implying the essence of roses. Shakespeare repeats the same idea and the same image elsewhere also, as in sonnet no. 5:

> But flow'rs distilled, though they with winter meet
> Leese but their show, thir substances still lives sweet.[8]

Nature images abound in this scene as well as in the rest of the play. Two features are to be noted. Important images related to nature can be found throughout the play which emphasize liquid elements. Lysander, for example, describes the time he and Hermia are to meet:

> Tomorrow night when Phoebe doth behold
> Her silver visage in the wat'ry glass,
> Decking with liquid pearl the bladed grass.[9]

Here there is reference to a body of water, (lake, pond or river) and to the dewdrops that cling to blades of grass. Referring to the many dew-images in the play C.L. Barber points out:

> Shakespeare's handling of nature has infused dew in this play with the vital spirit of moist and verdant woods.[10]

Besides images of flowers and trees there are numerous references to the image of the moon. There are six moon-images in the first scene alone. Caroline Spurgeon, referring to this wealth of moon-images, calls it:

> One of the earliest sustained effects of "iterative image."[11]

This is not only appropriate, but is to be expected in a play which is about a midsummer night. This "iterative" image helps to create the atmosphere of enchantment which is an essential part of the play. Imagery has ceased to be merely decorative and has become integral and also highly functional.

Not only animate images, but inanimate images of nature are also important in this play. In the moon-and-water image quoted above, the moon water and dewdrop—all are inanimate objects of nature, yet their effect is extremely strongly felt. The image of the lightning quoted earlier is also concerned with the inanimate aspect of nature. There are images of rain:

> Belike for want of rain, which I could well
> Beteem them from the tempest of my eyes.[12]

Here we have images of rain as well as of images of tempests—all inanimate, liquid, dynamic aspects of nature.

These images emphasize the effect of these inanimate objects on the world of human beings. Goethe, noting this, had remarked:

> Even the inanimate world takes part all the subordinate things have their role, the elements, the phenomena of the heavens, the earth and the sea, thunder and lightning.[13]

In this early play of Shakespeare the images are not so well-developed as they shall be later, yet, as in the passages quoted above, two inanimate aspects of nature, rain and tempest, serve to intensify the impact.

Apart from the animate and inanimate aspects of nature, there are images taken from different walks of life as well. Thus there are images taken from archery. Most appropriately the first of them is used by Hippolyta who herself, being an Amazon, was skilled in this branch of warfare:

> And then the moon, like to a silver bow
> New-bent in heaven.[14]

Usually the sliver of a new moon is compared with a boat. Hippolyta, being a warlike Amazonian, thinks of a bow. This image shows how Shakespeare, is already associating an image with the personality of the speaker. As has been pointed out by Clemen, as our poet's art developed, his use of imagery also became more and more complex. Of these, one line of development goes in the direction of suiting the image to the speaker. W. Clemen denies this feature to the early plays:

> We cannot speak of a true organic relationship of the image to the individual character who employs them.[15]

This might be true of the majority of the images in the *Dream*, but this image used by Hippolyta is definitely indicative of her own warlike personality.

Religious images are in frequent use in the play. In the first scene it is there in plentiful abundance. Theseus, explaining to Hermia that if she refuses to marry Demetrius as her father wishes, she will either have to face death or become a priestess of Diana:

> You can endure the livery of a nun,
> For aye to be in shady cloister mewed
> To live a barren sister all your life,
> Chanting faint hymns to the cold fruitless moon.[16]

Again, a few lines later he says:

> Or on Diana's alter to protest
> For aye, austerity and single life.[17]

Equally remarkable are two images used by Hermia, when she is lamenting their miserable plight in star-crossed love:

O cross! Too high to be enthralled to low
... ...
Because it is a customary cross.[18]

In both of these lines their misfortunes are being compared with a cross. What is to be kept in mind is that all these examples of religious images quoted above are Christian ones. Nuns and crosses belong to Christianity and are therefore quite unsuitable here, for the action of the *Dream* takes us to pagan times of ancient Greece. It is true that the vows of austerity and single life are required for becoming a priestess of Diana and therefore the image of a nun does not clash with pagan religious practices, but the image of the cross does and is therefore unacceptable to our highly trained modern sensibilities. The Elizabethan audience, however, was not so critical and would have taken such a glaring example of anachronism in its stride.

Shakespeare takes images from every walk of life. Just as he has made use of religious image, so has he made use of images from warfare, sport and other such activities. Thus in trying to make Hermia agree to bow to her father's will, Theseus tells her of the all-encompassing power of parents:

To whom you are but as a form in wax
By him imprinted, and within his power
To leave the figure or disfigure it.[19]

Here the image has been taken from the art of making moulds on soft wax so that statues or relief-work can be made out of them. Seals and coins also require copies made in wax as given here. There are, thus, images taken from different branches of knowledge, different professions, strewn throughout the play.

A very common feature of Shakespeare's poetry is the richness of effect produced by the accumulation of images. Like all the other aspects of his art this became more and more intensified as his technique matured. Even in an early play like this one, this feature can be seen:

Making it momentary as a sound,
Swift as a swallow, short as any dream,
Brief as the lightning in the collied night.[20]

Here Shakespeare has piled up no less than four images in three lines, each illustrating the same property of transitoriness. This speech is by Lysander and it has to be noted that each of the images are short and abstract. This makes the quality of transistoriness even more vivid.

It has been pointed out by W. Clemen that there is a significant difference between the images of the early plays and those of his mature plays. As his art developed his imagery became more and more functional. They became indicative of the character of the speaker, or became integrally related to the action of the play. This however is not the case with the early plays. Here the images are more decorative than functional. They are used to beautify the poetic style:

> The images in the early comedies elaborate, veil and adorn, but they do not yet elucidate.[21]

He does not discuss the imagery of the *Dream,* but this ornamental and decorative use of imagery can be early seen in many places. Thus when Hermia promises to meet Lysander the next night in the wood, she vows to do so with a host of images that overwhelm the reader by their richness and variety as well as their number. There are not many such passages in Shakespeare.

> I swear to thee by Cupid's strongest bow,
> By his best arrow with the golden head,
> By the simplicity of Venus's doves,
> By that which knitteth souls and prospers love,
> And by that fire which burned the carthage queen,
> When the false Troyan under sail was seen.[22]

Here each line makes use of a different image. This accumulation of images is not needed. It does not intensify, the effect, nor is it much functional. This passage gives the impression of artificiality and a rhetorical quality which calls attention to itself, its function being limited to Hermia's declaration of the strength of her love however, enhance the poetic style.

It will be seen that, in discussing the images of the play only those in the first scene of the first Act have been used. A thorough study of all the images in the entire play will make it clear to the diligent student how rich in imagery Shakespeare's poetry is. Even this one scene gives ample evidence of its wealth and variety.

(B) SYMBOLISM

Words and images and objects often have a symbolic dimension. Symbols go beyond the superficial meaning of the word or the object used and spread out to give it a wider as well as deeper significance. These have been classified into different categories by different writers. They have also been defined in many different ways. The definitions given by such poets as have used symbols themselves have special significance, as for example those given by Coleridge and Yeats. Coleridge for example, thinks that a symbol is organically linked with the thing for which it stands and is no more substitution. Several different characteristics of symbols have also been given by Coleridge.

Such definitions and classifications were not available to Shakespeare, for these are modern developments. This does not mean that such tools would be irrelevant if applied to him. On the contrary, they would enable us to understand and appreciate him all the better.

It is not that he made conscious and deliberate use of symbolism but many of the features of the plays are so deeply fraught with meaning that they have attained the status of symbols. Romances, specially, make use of symbols and the *Dream* is very much of a romance. Symbolism is usually seen as a feature of romances:

> Romance results from welcoming the strange and especially from welcoming the symbols, perforce fantastic, in which foreign lands, and far away ages have sought to express their intimations of immortality.[23]

It is not that there are many symbols in the *Dream,* but there are a few objects that have gained symbolic value. First of all there is the love-juice from the exotic flower:

... a little western flower;
Before, milk-white, now purple with love's wound
And maidens call it Love-in-Idleness.[24]

In other words it is the flower named pansy in modern English that he is talking about. The flower had received the gold-headed arrow of the god of love and ever since then has become a powerful love-potion. It is therefore symbolic of love. If the juice of this flower is dropped onto the eyelids of any sleeping person, then that person will fall violently in love with whatever being he or she sees on waking up:

The juice of it, on sleeping eyelids laid,
Will make or man or woman madly dote,
Upon the next live creature that it sees.[25]

The important factor here is that the one who receives the juice starts to "madly dote." In other words, it is a violent irrational kind of love. Many literary critics have talked about the many different kinds of love explored in this play and violent infatuation is one of them. The very name of the flower is Love-in-Idleness, that is, a quite frenzied kind of love. The flower and its juice thus symbolize a violent irrational love that fully controls a person.

Another important symbol in the play is Bottom's ass-head. As has been pointed out (*vide* Chap. 7., the character of Bottom, *supra*), this is a very complex symbol for it carries more than one meaning. Traditionally the ass is a well-known symbol for stupidity and in this play itself this has been emphasized many times:

(1) You see an ass-head of your own, do you?

(2) This is to make an ass-head of me, to fright me.

(3) Man is but an ass, if he go about to expound this dream.[26]

In all these instances the ass symbolizes stupidity. But this is not all, for the ass, from classical times, symbolizes sensuality as well.

> a fairly accessible interpretation sees it as the symbol for stupidity and sensuality, for the carnal man as opposed to the spiritual.[27]

From this point of view Bottom with his ass-head symbolizes both and it is ironical that it is the fairy queen, an ethereal figure, who is artificially made to fall in violent love with him.

The moon has been thought to be another symbol in the play. It has been referred to again and again. In the first scene itself there are six references to it. The moon stands as a symbol for Goddess Diana and thereby becomes a symbol for coldness and chastity. This is a holy quality, but it also implies sterility. Theseus refers to the moon twice to imply both of these traits:

> (1) Chanting faint hymns to the cold fruitless moon
>
> (2) Or on Diana's altar to protest
> For aye, austerity and single life.[28]

This symbolic value of the moon also has a paradoxical element in it, for it is by the light of the moon that the lovers meet. Thus the moon brings lovers together and is also the symbol of chastity.

The *Dream* is not a play rich in symbolism yet it is noticeable that, even in this early play the poet has already started to give symbolic depth to objects and images wherever possible. This tendency will grow as he develops and add splendour and glory to his mature poetry.

REFERENCES

1. Fluchère, H., *op. cit.* , p. 167.
2. *Ibid.*
3. Act I, sc. i, ll. 9-11, p. 33.
4. Act I, sc. i, ll. 30-31, p. 34.
5. Act I, sc. i, ll. 46-48, p. 37.
6. Clemen, W., *The Development of Shakespeare's Images,* Lond., Methuen, 1977, p. 187.
7. Act I, sc. i, ll. 76-78, p. 35.
8. Booth, Stephen, ed., *Shakespeare's Sonnets,* New Haven & London, Yale Univ. Press, 1977, p. 8.
9. Act I, sc. i, ll. 209-211, p. 38.

10. Barber, Cesar L., *May Games and Metamorphoses on a Midsummer Night*, in Price, A., *op. cit.*, p. 110.
11. *Ibid.*, p. 106.
12. Act I, sc. i, ll. 130-131, p. 36.
13. Quoted by Celmen, W., op. cit, p. 94.
14. Act I, sc. i, ll. 9-10, p. 33.
15. Clemen, *op. cit.*, p. 39.
16. Act I, sc. i, ll. 70-73, p. 35.
17. Act I, sc. i, ll. 89-90, p. 35.
18. Act I, sc. i, ll. 136 and 153, pp. 36-37.
19. Act I, sc. i, ll. 49-51, p. 34.
20. Act I, sc. i, ll. 143-145, p. 37.
21. Clemen, W., *op. cit.*, pp. 38-39.
22. Act I, sc. i, ll. 169-74, p. 37.
23. Whibley, Charles, ed., *George Wyndhan: Essays on Romantic Literature*, N.Y., 1968, p. 36.
24. Act II, sc. i, ll. 166-68, p. 47.
25. Act II, sc. i, ll. 170-72, p. 47.
26. (1) Act III, sc. i, l. 107, p. 58, (2) Act III, sc. i, ll. 110-11, p. 58. (3) Act IV, sc. i, ll. 204-05, p. 79.
27. Olson, Paul A., *op. cit.*, pp. 86-87.
28. Act I, sc. i, ll. 74-90, p. 35.

11

Poetic Style: Diction and Versification

This extremely important aspect of our poet's drama has been studied at great length. There are many aspects of poetic diction which, along with other elements, have served to make him the greatest English dramatist. Not only does his style reflect his age (i.e. it is an Elizabethan-Jacobean style), it reflects his personality as well. Again, the style is suited to each of the characters. Such achievements are little short of the miraculous.

Like all contemporary plays, Shakespeare's, also, were written in a mixture of prose and verse. The noble characters (usually those in the main plot) speak in verse and the humbler ones (usually in the sub-plots) speak prose. There, are many prose passages in our play, for the mechanicals' scenes are in prose. It should be borne in mind that poetic style has two clear-cut divisions: diction and versification. These two aspects shall be considered separately.

(A) POETIC DICTION

The Elizabethans were quite familiar with the classical theories of poetic diction, specially the theories of Roman writers. Horace had laid down the rules of poetic diction quite clearly in his *Ars Poetica.* The diction shall vary according to the genre of poetry and also according to the characters speaking. The diction for example, of elegies should be different from that of love-poems. In drama the characters should speak in conformity with their age, sex and social position:

> It will make a great difference whether a god or a hero is speaking, a man of ripe years or a hot-headed youngster

> in the pride of youth, a woman of standing or an officious nurse, a roving merchant or a prosperous farmer.[1]

This famous sentence has provided for all differences in the speeches of *dramatis personae* of all kinds. First of all, distinction is made between the divine and the human. Among human beings there are hundreds of varieties and diction must be adjusted to all these. Age must be taken into account ("man of ripe years or a hot-headed youngster") and so must sex ("woman of standing"). Within these basic categories there are many other divisions according to age and social status. Horace differentiates between "a woman of standing or an officious nurse." A classic example of such a duo is that of Lady Capulet and the Nurse in *Romeo and Juliet*. He also differentiates among the different professions: "roving merchant" and a "prosperous farmer." These categories can be added to *ad infinitum*. In other words the language should suit the speaker. Accordingly, in later Elizabethan drama, diction became highly specialized. As M.C. Bradbrook has pointed out:

> The specific style for princes, for lovers, for clowns, was fixed.[2]

Certain things, however, should in general be kept in mind by the poet—whichever variety of style he might be using. Not only must the diction be realistic in accordance with the speaker's personality, it must also be such as to persuade the reader or the audience and at the same time move his feeling:

> The Elizabethan dramatist's style is one of impassioned poetic rhetoric, the two commonest functions of which are to persuade and to touch the emotions.[3]

Classical theorists have also pointed out that a poet should make use of rhetorical figures. Aristotle points out, in the definition of tragedy, the indispensable part of poetic diction. The style may be the grand, or the middle or the low style, according to the content of the work or the nature of the speaker, but it should make use of rhetorical embellishments. Ben Jonson's masterly work *The Alchemist* is an ideal example. The low style has been used here, as the main characters come from the lowest rungs of the social ladder, but when the only aristocrat in the play, Sir Epicure Mammon, speaks Jonson switches over to the grand style with effortless ease and this is expected—it does not give rise to a feeling of incongruity. But, whether it is Sir Epicure who is speaking, or Face the servant, Jonson uses figures of speech in both the cases.

English theorists, also, have followed the classical theorists, and recommended the use of figures of speech. George Puttenham the Elizabethan rhetorician had said:

> There is nothing so little for the poem as to be furnished with al the figures that be Rhetoricall and such as do most beautifie the language with eloquence.[4]

Many other theories have been advanced by the classical and later rhetoricians. Horace, for example, tells the would-be poet to use newly-coined words as well as out-of-mode words which should be given a new lease of life. Shakespeare was fully acquainted with these ideas and had used them, according to his discretion, making his style rich and intense.

(i) Diction in the Dream

As can be seen in the chronological table, Shakespeare's dramatic career stretches over quite a long period (*vide* Ch. 3, *supra*), i.e. over two decades. This is a period of continuous development for him. His art strode over new territories as the years passed and riper years reached higher peaks of excellence. Not only did his art of characterization and plot management develop, but so did his style and of course, versification. The *Dream* is an early play and in it he has employed a diction eminently suited to the kind of play it is—a romantic comedy with fairy-tale elements in it. No wonder that G.K. Chesterton had declared:

> In pure poetry and the intoxication of words, Shakespeare never rose higher than he rises in this play.[5]

Moreover, he adopts all the conventions of style as obtained in Elizabethan drama and shows how they can be used to serve his own artistic purposes. The use of a mixture of prose and verse serves to distinguish the noble from the humble characters, as is to be found in all Elizabethan drama. Moreover, it was also one of the requirements of poetic diction that the language should be in harmony with the action taking place on the stage. This is what Aristotle has to say in this context:

> ... language enriched in a variety of ways and artistic devices appropriate to the several parts of the play.[6]

This indicates that even the same character must not speak in the same manner in different situations. Lysander speaks in soft but elevated style when talking to Hermia in the first scene, and later when quarrelling with her after his eyes have been doctored by Puck uses violent and abusive language. Hermia herself, protesting her willingness to meet Lysander in the forest, speaks in highly elevated allusive style. Yet later when Lysander has forsaken her for Helena she abuses the later like a fishwife. The language used by the fairies is specially remarkable for its beauty and lightness. Some of the stylistic devices employed in the play shall now be studied.

(ii) Stylistic Devices

There are many kinds of stylistic devices that a poet can command. Of these, imagery, symbols and figures of speech are the most important ones. The two former have already been studied, however sketchily, in the preceding chapter. A few of the most important figures of speech used by the poet shall now be taken up. As was done in the case of imagery, some of the figures in Act I, sc. i, shall be pointed out.

Similes are usually the most easily discernible figures of speech, and they are present almost everywhere in the play. Thus in the very first two speeches by Theseus and Hippolyta, similes are used to describe the moon. Theseus uses a simile with negative associations most effectively:

> Theseus: She lingers my desires,
> Like to a step-dame, or a dowager,
> Long withering out a young man's revenue.[7]

and then, in answer to this grumbling, Hippolyta uses a martial simile to describe the same moon:

> And then the moon, like to a silver bow
> New-bent in heaven, shall behold the night
> Of our solemnities.[8]

Two such similes one succeeding the other, both describing the same object yet so different in tone make it clear how very versatile and flexible Shakespeare's imagination was.

Accumulated or extended simile is also a well-known feature of Shakespeare's poetry and a good example of this figure of speech is to be found in the first scene. It occurs when Lysander, exemplifying the impermanence of love, uses four similes in quick succession. This is a very effective passage of Shakespeare's early poetry and has already been mentioned:

> Making it momentary as a sound,
> Swift as a shadow, short as any dream,
> Brief as the lightning in the collied night.[9]

Each of these similes is effective for each illustrates transitoriness. A sound, a shadow, a dream and a lightning-flash, all are brief and evanescent. The last simile, moreover, is carried on for a few more lines and can be taken as an example of a Homeric simile:

> Brief as the lightning in the collied night
> That (in a spleen) unfolds both heaven and earth,
> And, ere a man hath power to say "Behold!"
> The jaws of darkness do devour it up.[10]

This four-line simile is neatly concluded at the end by pin-pointing the moral and uniting all:

> So quick bright things come to confusion.[11]

This is a proof of the exuberance of Shakespeare's imagination as well as his instinctive orderliness—a passage of three accumulated similes, followed by a Homeric simile and all neatly tied up at the end by pointing out a general truth that applies to all four of them.

Metaphors have, since classical times, been taken seriously as an extremely important and effective rhetorical device. Shakespeare is a master of this figure of speech. Instances of metaphors, sometimes clear and emphatic, sometimes hidden and implicit, sometimes frozen, sometimes mixed, are strewn everywhere. One of the finest metaphors is used by Theseus when he is explaining the difference between a married woman and a single one:

> But earthlier happy is the rose distilled,
> Than that which, withering on the virgin thorn,
> Grows, lives and dies in single blessedness.[12]

Actually there are two metaphors here, as corresponding to two types of women. The married woman is compared with a rose whose sweet essence is used in perfume and lives on for a long time, imparting delight to others. The single woman is, on the other hand, like a rose that withers on its stalk without serving any purpose.

Another metaphor, a more complex one, has been used by Helena at the end of the scene. She is talking or ,rather, soliloquizing, about the inconstancy of Demetrius, who used to be her own sweetheart before he had met Hermia. His vows of love made at that time are being compared with hail:

> And when this hail some heat from Hermia felt,
> So he dissolved, and showr's oath did melt.[13]

So here the love-vows of Demetrius are like hail (i.e. bits of ice) which melted when he came into contact with Hermia's beauty and turned into a shower of rain. Here we have a simile which is a dynamic one, for a change from hail to rain is given. It is also a simile making use of inanimate objects of nature and also one that uses transformation of an element into a different state i.e. from solid to liquid.

Synecdoche is not a figure of speech which is an obvious one, springing automatically to the eye. Shakespeare uses it quite often. Thus Egeus accuses Lysander of having cunningly made his daughter fall in love with him:

> This man hath bewitched the bosom of my child.[14]

Here the bosom which is a concrete object, is being substituted for the heart or the emotions, which are abstract, thus affording an example of synecdoche.

Antithesis is a figure which adds piquancy and incisiveness to poetry and Shakespeare uses it quite often. Thus in the very beginning of the first scene Theseus, addressing Hippolyta, says:

Hippolyta, I wooed thee with my sword
and won thy love, doing thee injuries.[15]

Here the idea of winning love by hurting contains contradiction within itself, but the antithetical quality is not as clear as is desirable. Later on in other instances it becomes far more distinct:

Her: I frown upon him, yet he loves me still.
Hel.: O that your frown would teach my smiles such skill!
Her: I give him curses, yet he gives me love.
Hel: O that my prayers could such affection move !
Her: The more I hate the more he follows me
Hel: The more I love, the more he hateth me.[16]

This is a very good example of antithesis. Here we have antitheses in each individual line and alternate lines are antithetical in relation to each other. Hermia's sentences are antithetical in themselves and then Helena's answers contradict hers. There is thus an interweaving of antitheses in the lines spoken by the two girls.

Rhetorical questions add dynamic quality to poetry and our poet makes use of this figure of speech to very good purpose in this scene. Thus Lysander addresses Hermia as soon as the two elders have left the stage:

How now, my love? Why is your cheek so pale?
How chance the roses there do pale so fast?[17]

Here we have three questions—questions which do not need answers, in two lines. It is true that Hermia does answer them in the next line but actually it is not necessary to do so, Lysander knows very well why she is looking so pale. The questions, however, highlight his solicitude.

Exclamation is another figure of speech that gives an all-round elevation as well as dynamic quality to blank verse. A series of exclamations occur in this scene:

Her: O cross! Too high to be enthralled to low
Lys: Or else misgrafted in respect of years-
Her: O spite! Too old to be engaged to young.
L.: Or else it stood upon the choice of friends—

H: O hell! To choose love by another's eyes!
L.: Or, if there were a sympathy in choice.[18]

The first line of this dialogue contains, besides an exclamation, also a metonymy. The cross, the symbol for the burden of suffering, has been substituted for the thing symbolised, i.e. the suffering she is undergoing.

Personification is a common figure of speech in the grand style, for it gives sublimity to language, Shakespeare uses it in this scene to give concreteness to the concepts he wants to convey. Helena thus gives a well-known personification of love:

Things base and vile, holding no quantity,
Love can transpose to form and dignity.[19]

This personification goes on for eight more lines. The entire figure of speech thus covers a total of ten lines, and such long examples are very rare.

This sketchy account shows that Shakespeare has used a great wealth of rhetorical figures in this first scene alone, yet there are many that do not occur here though they are repeatedly used later. One such figure is very important in this play but it has not been used even once in this scene. This is the figure of malapropism. It occurs times without number in many scenes later on, specially in those concerning the mechanicals. A few examples will be enough. Thus, in Act III sc. i which is the rehearsal scene in the forest, Bottom commits a malapropism and then Quince corrects him:

B: "Thisby, the flowers have odious savours sweet"
Q: Odours: "oderous."[20]

Later when Bottom wakes up after the ass-head has been taken away he tries to explain the indescribable quality of his experience and uses a number of malapropisms. The passage is a well-known one, a parody of a Biblical passage (*vide* Ch. 7, Bottom's character, *supra*). Referring to these malapropisms C. Watts has remarked:

His malapropisms brightly glow with symbolisms.[21]

Apart from figures of speech there are many other stylistic devices poets use to make their style effective. Allusion is one of them. These can be of many kinds: popular allusions, topical allusions, mythical, Biblical, etc. One finds many such in this play. Quite early in the first scene, in the very opening speech of Theseus there is one:

> four happy days bring in
> Another moon: but O/me thinks how slow
> This old moon wanes![22]

Theseus and Hippolyta are to be married when the new moon is in the sky. This refers to a popular belief that marriages performed during the new moon nights were lucky and happy.

Topical allusions are always loved by audiences and a remarkable topical allusion occurs in Act II sc. i when Oberon describes how he saw Cupid's gold arrow falling on a flower:

> a certain aim he took
> At a fair vestal, throned by the west.[23]

but Cupid's fiery arrow was dampened by the cold moonlight and missed its mark. Cupid's intended victim remained unaffected:

> And the imperial vot'ress passed on
> In maiden meditation, fancy-free.[24]

The 'fair vestal' and the 'imperial vot'ress' is actually Queen Elizabeth. Attempts had been made to interest her in proposals of marriage but she was indifferent to them. Shakespeare thus calls her a priestess of Diana who is the Goddess of chastity.

The most famous Biblical allusion in this play of course is Bottom's speech at the end of Act IV, sc. i:

> I have had a most rare vision.... The eye of man hath not heard, the ear of man hath not seen, man's hand is not able to taste, his tongue to conceive, nor his heart to report, what my dream was.[25]

This refers to St. Paul's first Epistle to the Corinthians, where the apostle is talking of mystical experiences vouchsafed unto saints:

> Eye hath not seen, nor ears heard, neither have entered

> into the heart of man, the things which God hath prepared for them that love him.[26]

Bottom's speech, of course, is a comic parody of a serious passage, yet it can be definitely classed as a Biblical allusion that would have been easily recognized by the audience.

Classical allusions are extremely common in all poetry and as this play is about ancient Greece it is but natural that there should be many such. The playlet of Pyramus and Thisby is itself a classical myth. Apart from that there are numerous classical allusions. In the first scene itself there are six mythical allusions, three of them occurring in a speech by Hermia protesting her sincerity:

> I swear to thee by Cupid's strongest bow,
> By the simplicity of Venus' doves
> By that which knitteth souls and prospers loves,
> And by that fire which burned the Carthage queen
> When the false Troyan under sail was seen.[27]

Here Cupid the God of love, Venus the Goddess of love, Dido, one of the most famous victims of tragic love and Aeneas her lover—all are brought together within five lines. Though Shakespeare often gives instances of accumulation of figures of speech and images, instances of accumulated mythical allusion are not so common.

These are only a few of the rhetorical devices employed by the dramatist to intensify the effects of his style. Close analysis will reveal many more.

(B) VERSIFICATION

It has been pointed out at the very outset that diction and versification are but two sides of the same coin—poetic style. Any discussion of a poet's style is incomplete unless both of these aspects are dealt with. A knowledge of prosody is essential for understanding versification, which is a highly technical aspect of poetry. Henri Fluchère says:

> It is by its rhythm as much as by its images that a verse is expressive. The rhythmical succession has an emotional patterns, shows a purpose, imposing a mood or defining a thought.[28]

The basic poetical form used on Elizabethan drama is blank verse. This form consists of lines of unrhymed iambic pentametres. The iambic measure is a disyllabic measure of which the initial syllable is unstressed and the second one is stressed. Each line contains five such feet. Given below is an example of regular blank verse from Theseus's speech in the first scene:

> Tak̆e tíḿe / tŏ paúse / ăňd bý / thĕ néxt / neŵ móon /
>
> Th̆e séa / iňg – dáy / bĕtwi̊xt / m̆y lóv́e / ăňd ḿe /
>
> Fŏr é /vĕrlas̀t / iňg bónd / of̆ fé / llŏwshíp /
>
> Ŭpón / thăt dáy / ĕithér / prĕpáre / tŏ díe /[29]

This passage has four lines, with no rhymes of any kind. All the lines are iambic pentametres. Such absolutely regular blank verse passages are difficult to find. There are usually other metres like trochees and anapaests, mixed with the iambs to give flexibility to a passage of blank verse.

There are many complex features of versification. Two such features are the use of end-stopped and of run-on lines. The former is the kind of line that requires the reader (or the actor) to make a definite pause at the end. Elizabethan plays of early times usually had end-stopped blank verse and this made such verse mechanical and monotonous as well as rather jerky instead of smooth. Thus in one of the well-known pre-Shakespearean play *Fulgens and Lucrece* by Henry Medwall the heroine says:

> Nay, nay, sir, that guise is best,
> Ye cannot displease me withal;
> And according to your desire I shall,
> Even as soon as I goodly may,
> Answer you therein without delay.[30]

Every line in this passage has a comma or some such punctuation mark at the end which will make the actor pause. In cases like this the verse gives an impression of being stilted and clumsy. At times, however, end stopped lines can be used deliberately for a specific purpose, as for example to emphasize certain lines or ideas. Shakespeare has used them with great effect in Egeus's speech in the first scene. He is accusing Lysander of having cunningly made Hermia fall in love with him:

Thou, Lysander, thou hast given her rhymes,
And inter-change love-tokens with my child;
Thou hast by moonlight, at her window sung,
With feigning voice, verses of faining love.[31]

Here Shakespeare has made the lines end-stooped ones in order to emphasize each of the lines. Each line is like a blow of the hammer, very emphatic.

On the other hand, we have run-on lines which are also known as enjambements. Here, there is no stopping at the end of the line. Instead the lines flow smoothly into the next. Most good blank verse is of this kind. The very opening lines that are spoken by Theseus are a good example:

Now, fair Hippolyta our nuptial hour
Draws on apace: four happy days bring in
Another moon but O methinks how slow
This old moon wanes![32]

Here the actor does not have to pause at the end. Instead he moves on to the next line, pausing in order to take breath somewhere within the line. This makes the verse smooth and natural.

Pausing somewhere in the middle of the line is technically known as the caesura or the medial pause. Prior to the development of Elizabethan blank verse mediaeval verse had a special feature; it had a pause in the middle of the line. This may be seen in the poetry of Langland and others. This too made for a very jerky rhythm. Shakespeare and other Elizabethan writers varied the placing of the caesura from line to line so that the passage may have some flexibility. Thus Theseus speaks a highly flexible blank verse here:

Either to die the death, // or to abjure
For ever // the society of men
Therefore, fair Hermia // question your desires
Know of your youth //examine well your blood.[33]

Here the double vertical lines indicate the caesura. In the first line the caesura falls after the sixth syllable and in the second after the third. Again, in the third line it falls after the fifth and in the fourth line after the fourth syllable. Thus the actor shall stop for breath at different places in different lines. This makes for smooth and natural delivery.

Very often, for greater effect the writer may make use of more than one caesura in the same line. Thus in the lines given below there is more than just one caesura for special purposes:

> But // being ever-full of self-affection,
> My mind did lose it // But, // Demetrius, // come,
> And come, // Egeus // you shall go with me.[34]

Here the first line contains one caesura after the first syllable. The next line has three of them, one after the fifth, and the second after the sixth and the third after the ninth syllable likewise the third line has two caesurae, the first after the second syllable and the next after the fourth. All this variation makes for a smooth and utterly natural dialogue.

Blank verse contains ten syllables by its very nature but this rule is not a hard and fast one. Very often, in order to vary the monotony of the lines the writer may use more, or less, than ten syllables:

> F̆or évĕr thé sŏcíetў ŏf mén[35]

This line has nine syllables instead of ten and the following line has eleven:

> Ă góod pĕrsúasĭon: thérefŏre héar m̆e Hérmĭa[36]

Another way, of introducing variety in blank verse is the use of stichomythia. One variety of this occurs when there are quick, single line exchanges of dialogues between different characters:

> Hermia: O cross! Too high to be enthralled to low.
> Lys: Or else misgraffèd in respect of years—
> H: O Spite ! Too old to be engaged to young.
> L.: Or else it stood upon the choice of friends—

H.: O hell ! To choose one by another's eyes ![37]

Here the two characters cap each other's lines. A more intricate variety of stichomythia can be seen when the one and the same line is broken up:

Hermia: So is Lysander.
Theseus: In himself he is.[38]

Here a line of ten syllables is broken up to accommodate two speakers. An extreme example of this occurs later in the play when a line is broken up into five parts and distributed among four speakers:

Peaseblossom: Ready
Cobweb: And I—
Moth: And I—
Mustardseed And I—
All four: Where shall we go?[39]

This line is a hexametre, that is, it has six feet and twelve syllables. As it is broken up among no less than four speakers, the length passes unnoticed.

Apart from blank verse, couplets are also used in these plays. This one, in particular, contains long passages of couplets. There are, for example, forty couplets in the first scene alone. In Act II sc. i. there are thirty-five. The next scene contains forty-eight of them. The second scene of Act III, which is the longest in the play, has a hundred and seven couplets. These are all ten-syllable couplets, i.e. heroic couplets:

O He / len, god / ess, nymph / perfect / divine!
To what / my love / shall I / compare / thine eyne?
Crystal / is mud / dy, O, / how ripe / in show.
Thy lips / those kiss / ing che / rries, tempt / ing grow.[40]

Very often these heroic couplets used to give a comic touch, as has been done here. Sometimes, as in the last lines spoken by Theseus it is used to make a solemn announcement:

A fortnight hold we this solemnity,
In nightly revels and new jollity.[41]

In addition to heroic couplets, this play has many octosyllabic couplets as well. These passages occur mainly as chants by Oberon and Puck. There are many of these, mostly in trochaic metre.

Apart from these features there are also songs. There are nine songs besides those in the playlet. In the playlet there are three of them. Of the others, two are sung by Bottom. In fact he has the honour of singing the first song in the play. The others are all sung by the fairies. These are some of the finest songs by Shakespeare, particularly the one sung by the fairy in Act II sc. i, and the Lullaby sung to put Titania to sleep. Both of them, in fact, are such songs as show Shakespeare's familiarity with country flowers and animals. Thus in the first song the fairy singing it says:

> The cowslips tall her pensioners be;
> In their gold coats spots you see:
> These be rubies, fairy favours;
> In those freckles live their savours.[42]

In the Lullaby the humble country animals to be found in England are mentioned:

> You spotted snakes with double tongue,
> Thorny hedgehogs, be not seen,
> Newts and blind-worms, do no wrong:
> Come not near our fairy queen.[43]

Bottom's song is nothing so much as a catalogue of birds. He mentions six birds in eight lines. It is a fine description of these homely birds. It is not a parody but a colourful and graphic description worthy of wakening Titania from her slumbers.

The three songs in the playlet are hilarious parodies of the bombastic and melodramatic diction affected by many poets of the time and afford an instance of comic laughter:

> But stay: O spite!
> But mark, poor knight,
> What dreadful dole is here!
> Eyes, do you see?

How can it be?
O dainty duck, O dear![44]

Music, both vocal and instrumental, often plays a very important part in Shakespeare's plays. This is an early play and in it music does not have the significance it has, for example, in the *Tempest*. Even then, it serves to create the proper atmosphere in this play and above everything else, it serves a certain purpose that it does in no other play, for here we have songs that are parodies and provide comic laughter.

The different aspects of poetic style, as have been sketchily dealt with, form one facet of the play. In this chapter all the examples of figures of speech and metre have been taken from one scene only, Act I, sc i, as had been done with the images in the preceding chapter. The earnest student will realise what variety and wealth of imagery and rhetoric can be found in the rest of the play. It is not surprising that G.K. Chesterton should declare:

> In pure poetry and the intoxication of words, Shakespeare never rose higher than he rises in this play.[45]

REFERENCES

1. Dorsch, T.S., ed. and transl., *Classical Literary Criticism*, Penguin Books, 1975, p. 83.
2. Bradbrook, M.C., *op. cit.*, p. 45.
3. Fluchère, H., *op. cit.*, p. 152.
4. Quoted by Fluchère, *op. cit.*, p. 159.
5. Chesterton, G.K., in Price, *op. cit.*, p. 43.
6. Dorsch, T.S., *op. cit.*, p. 39.
7. Act I, sc. i, ll. 4-6, p. 33.
8. Act I, sc. i, ll. 9-11, p. 33.
9. Act I, sc. i, ll. 143-45, p. 37.
10. Act I, sc. i, ll. 145-48, p. 37.
11. Act I, sc. i, l. 149, p. 37.
12. Act I, sc. i, ll. 76-78, p. 35.
13. Act I, sc. i, ll. 244-45, p. 39.
14. Act I, sc. i, l. 26, p. 34.
15. Act I, sc. i, ll. 16-17, p. 33.

16. Act I, sc. i, ll. 194-99, p. 38.
17. Act I, sc. i, ll. 128-29, p. 36.
18. Act I, sc. i, ll. 136-41, p. 36.
19. Act I, sc. i, ll. 232-33, p. 39.
20. Act III, sc. i, ll. 73-74, p. 57.
21. Watts, C., *op. cit.*, p. 16.
22. Act I, sc. i, ll. 2-5, p. 33.
23. Act II, sc. i, ll. 157-58, p. 47.
24. Act II, sc. i, ll. 163-64, p. 47.
25. Act IV, sc. i, ll. 203-11, pp. 79-80.
26. I Corinthians, 2:9. *The Holy Bible,* American Bible Society, New York, no date, p. 170.
27. Act I, sc .i, ll. 169-74, p. 37.
28. Fluchere, H., *op. cit.*, p. 181.
29. Act I, sc. i, ll. 83-86, p. 35.
30. Boas, F.S., ed., *Five Pre-Shakespearean Plays, OUP,* 1934, p. 19.
31. Act I, sc. i, ll. 28-31, p. 34.
32. Act I, sc. i, ll. 1-4, p. 33.
33. Act I, sc. i, ll. 65-68, p. 35.
34. Act I, sc. i, ll. 113-15, p. 36.
35. Act I, sc. i, l. 66, p. 35.
36. Act I, sc. i, l. 156, p. 37.
37. Act I, sc. i, ll. 136-40, p. 36.
38. Act I, sc. i, l. 53, p. 34.
39. Act III, sc i, l. 9, p. 59.
40. Act III, sc. ii, ll. 137-140, p. 64.
41. Act V, sc. i, ll. 353-54, p. 92.
42. Act II, sc. i, ll. 10-13, p. 43.
43. Act II, sc. ii, ll. 9-12, p 50.
44. Act V, sc. i, ll. 263-69, p. 89.
45. Price, A., *op. cit.*, p. 43.

12

Critical Reception

A Midsummer Night's Dream was a highly popular play in its time, but, as the centuries rolled on and Shakespeare's works came to be evaluated more and more seriously, this play was gradually relegated to the background as one of his early and minor plays. Yet it is an acknowledged fact that it is the last of his early plays. G.K. Chesterton, as a matter of fact, goes to the extent of saying, with reference to this play:

> The greatest of Shakespeare's comedies is also, from a certain point of view, the greatest of his plays.[1]

Certain facts about this play, which do not come under any of the heads that have been discussed so far, will now have to be clarified before a start can be made on the study of the history, or rather the critical history of the play. First of all it is well-known that the play was performed in order to celebrate a royal, or at any rate a noble, marriage. For a long time it was not known exactly which marriage it was. John Dover Wilson, for example, had given seven possible occasions which he had taken from E.K. Chambers and had added another from a different source. After having had a look at all seven, he fixed on the fourth in the list:

> I now suggest that Shakespeare's play was performed at yet a third wedding, that of Thomas Berkely to Elizabeth Carey at Blackfriars on 19th February, 1596.[2]

This is the opinion that has endured till now. It is also known that it had become a popular play and had been acted several times:

> The title-page of the 1600 Quarto informs us that it had been "sundry times publickely acted by the Right honourable the Lord Chamberlaine his servants."[3]

Later on the play was altered and acted many times more. It is a known fact that nine different texts had been published up to 1816, some of which were based entirely on music. The original version was restored in 1840. Many stage-effects were produced by the nineteenth century stage managers which had not been possible earlier. Gas lighting and, later, electricity, revolutionized stage-lighting, making moonlight and dawn effects possible. Mendelssohn's music added a new dimension to late Victorian productions, with the introduction of ballet-sequences. This in turn needed ballet costumes, for fairies with transparent wings did not exist in Elizabethan times. All these stage-effects were not approved by Hazlitt:

> All that is fine in the play was lost in representation. The spectacle was grand, but the spirit was evaporated, the genius was fled.[4]

This happened because the stage-manager aimed at realism. The middle of the nineteenth century saw the same trouble. There was, for example, Charles Kean's production in1856 in which the backdrop had consisted of:

> ... an elaborate and undoubtedly most beautiful bird's eye view of Athens as it was in the time of Pericles.[5]

This critic also objects to a fanciful spectacle in the second Act. One of the special advertisements on the play-bill was "Titania's Shadow Dance." Henry Morley was highly offended at the concept for it is a well-known fact that supernatural beings do not cast shadows:

> Of all things in the world, a shadow-dance of fairies! If anything in the way of an effect of light was especially desirable, it should have been such an arrangement as would have made the fairies appear to be dancing in a light so managed as to cast no shadows, and give them true spiritual attributes.[6]

Thus this production was too realistic from one point of

view in presenting a spectacle of Periclean Athens, yet on the other hand not realistic enough because it presented shadows of beings who do not cast shadows.

Towards the end of the nineteenth century there was a production of which the review was written by Shaw. By this time electricity was available. All the fairies were fitted with portable batteries and lights which they continually switched on and off. The use of a trapeze was also made for Puck. It is ironical that nearly a hundred years later, in 1970, trapezes were used again, and this time not just for Puck, but for other characters also. The craze for realism continued thus, into the twentieth century, for later productions also stressed this factor.

It is said that in 1900, Sir Herbert Beerbohm Tree had brought real oak trees, live deer, pigeon, rabbits, squirrels and hares on the stage and this was strongly resented by the actors because these got more attention from the audience than the actors themselves.

The twentieth century has seen many innovations in many fields and Shakespeare's plays have always provided the basis for many experiments. H. Granville-Barker's production in 1914 became a subject for controversy:

> The production aroused furious controversy. To some it was too metallic to the eye and too insufferably melodious to the ear. One or two people suspected that those gilded sprites were the creations of a man who did not believe in fairies.... The challenge to tradition was too strident.[7]

An extreme was reached in 1970 by Peter Brooks. This production was remarkable for its stage-sets and props, all of which were designed by Sally Jacobs. John Russell Brown has given a description of this set. First of all she had put a three-sided white box on the stage. Inside this artificially reduced acting-space the actual performance was held. Around the box and above it there was a lot of space in which music was played. Stage tricks were prepared, the actors got ready for their scenes, in full view of the audience. All the stage-props were strange, unexpected and unrealistic. There were circus props like trapezes by which the characters entered and left the stage. Coiled wires were used to represent trees. Black metal ladders were placed on each side of the stage at front on which the actors climbed and acted. All these and many more features made the entire thing deliberately unreal:

> By creating a kind of clean, stark gymnasium or circus for the setting of this production the director and the designer ignored many of the words of the text, especially the ambiguous, gentle and homely words in which the play abounds.[8]

The most recent production of the play was held in 2006. Produced by Tim Supple, it was performed in seven languages with only about half of it in English. It was called "an Indian production" and "the most life-enhancing production of Shakespeare's play since Peter Brook's." Tim Supple was commissioned by the British Council in India and Sri Lanka to stage this Indian version. He collected together twenty-three dancers, musicians, actors and performers and the production itself was in English, Tamil, Bengali, Hindi, Malaysian, Sinhalese, Marathi, and a little Sanskrit. How much of this multilingual production was also Shakespearean is subject to doubt.

On the stage, thus, the play has been very popular, for it gives great opportunities to directors and stage-managers. It presents many challenges to them, particularly in the fairies and Bottom's ass-head. The latter has been presented in many fanciful ways.

Literary criticism, however, has not been equally favourable. Samuel Pepys, in his famous *Diary*, mentions it with disapproval:

> ... to the King's Theatre, where we saw *A Midsummer Night's Dream*, which I had never seen before, nor shall ever again, for it is the most insipidly ridiculous play that ever I saw in my life.[9]

This hostile attitude has been defended and explained by John Middleton Murry. According to him the three chief elements of the play, that is, the theme of love, the fairies and the clowning, were much too simple and childish for a polished man of the world like Pepys. On the other hand he was not sophisticated enough for the bringing together of all these three elements, which resulted in a rare combination which only a specialised intellectual would appreciate and approve.

Serious literary criticisms can be found in Dr. Johnson's notes on the play as well as in his Prefaces to Shakespeare. He comments on the individual scenes, some of which have been already quoted in the appropriate context (*Vide* Ch. 5, *Scene-wise Analysis, supra*). Then in his general comments on the play he says:

> Wild and fantastic as the play is, all the parts in their various modes are well-written and give the kind of pleasure which the author designed.[10]

Much more memorable is his comment on the localization of the action in different places, i.e., the forest and Theseus's palace. (*vide* Ch. 9, Plot, the section on the unity of place, *supra*).

Criticism underwent a most important change in its very basics in the nineteenth century, with the arrival of the Romantic poets. They laid stress on the exploration of psychological depths and also on the depiction of emotions. Thus Hazlitt observes:

> It has been observed that Shakespeare's characters are constructed upon deep psychological principles; and there is something in this play which is very like it.[11]

In the twentieth century literary critics started to analyze different aspects of the play, like the theme, the art of characterization, the individual characters, the plot-structure, the style, etc. These features had been commented upon earlier also, but detailed studies had not been made. Revival of interest in many Elizabethan elements, like Elizabethan psychology, philosophy and cosmology has led to analyses of the plays from these points of views as well. Thus Minor White Latham has made a special study of Elizabethan beliefs in fairies and studies the fairies of this play from this point of view. He comes to many important conclusions. For example he says that Shakespeare has presented the fairies in a manner totally different from that of earlier writers, for he had made them benevolent towards mankind:

> For the first time the fairies themselves are made consistently good. No longer do they function as the mischievous and dangerous beings they were believed to be.... They become in actuality, the Good Neighbours.[12]

The sources from which the poet had taken the material for his plays had always intrigued literary critics and G. Bullough made a thorough study of these. His work in this field is not only a pioneering work but an authoritative one also. He has found no less than eleven sources for this play which have been mentioned in the relevant place (*vide* Ch. 9, the section on Sources, *supra*).

Many branches of Elizabethan beliefs have been used to interpret the play. William Rossky for example studies the renaissance attitude to the human imagination and interprets the play accordingly. Slightly different from this is the study of the use of imagination by R.W. Dent.

The imagery of Shakespeare's play has been studied by Caroline Spurgeon and W. Clemen and they have paid more attention to the major plays than to this one. Their brief comments show that though the imagery is rich and complex it operates at a more superficial level than it does in the mature plays. Here the imagery is more decorative than functional.

Late twentieth century brought forth many critical essays following the methods of the numerous new schools of criticism that have sprung up recently—like structuralism, formalism, hermeneutics, etc. Indian writers have tried to interpret it according to Indian theories. One such attempt shall now be given, studying the play from the viewpoint of Indian dramaturgy and the rasavāda.

INDIAN DRAMATURGY

According to Indian dramatic theory, there are ten kinds of rūpakas. The most authentic work in this field is Ācārya Dhananjaya's Daśa-rūpaka and he has clearly said that this classification has been done while keeping in mind three factors: the content, the character and the *angīrasa* in mind.

> Vastu, netā, rasāṣṭesāṅ bhedako vastu ca tridhā.[13]

That is to say, the subject-matter, the hero and the rasas—the difference in these three give rise to the difference among the *rūpakas* or the plays.

According to this division the *Dream* will be a nātikā. In such plays the narrative content or *vastu* may be *utpādya* or imaginary. The story of the play is not entirely original to Shakespeare but it is not, on the other hand, as well-known as a myth or a Biblical story. The playlet of course is *prakhyāta*, but it is not the real or the main play. Moreover, though the poet took the different plots from different sources, yet he altered them in many ways and finally welded them together to form a new play. The two heroes Lysander and Demetrius are not *prakhyāta* heroes like the ones from epics, or a historical figure. Thus they too are utpādya. Theseus is a *prakhyāta* figure but he is not the hero.

The main or the angirasa of a nātikā should be Śrngra or the erotic rasa and there is scope for debate in this matter. The main as well as the two sub-plots whether comic or fairy-plot, both have the element of śṛṅgāra in them. Love is the over-riding theme and a triple marriage is the outcome. Śṛṅgāra *rasa*, as used in the play fulfills the three conditions necessary for the angī-rase like *vahuvyāpti*, *phalāgama*, etc. But here a dispute might arise because this is a play in which the adbhūta rasa is equally important. Indeed, it might be said that it is the *angī* of the play. If we analyse the individual scenes from this point of view we get the following data:

Adbhūta	*Śṛṅgāra*	Both
Act III, sc. i	Act I, sc. i	Act II, sc. i & ii
Act IV, sc. i		Act III sc. i, Act V, i.

This shows that *Adbhūta* rasa is at least as important in the play as *Śṛṅgāra*. So the question of *vahuvyāpti* is answered. As far as *phalāgama* is concerned, when one thinks of the overall impression of the play as a whole the lovers pale into insignificance and what one does remembers are the antics of the fairies. These are complex issues but a detailed analysis will make us arrive at this conclusion. So it is difficult to say what is the *angī rasa* of the play, *Śṛṅgāra* or *adbhūta*. It depends upon the individual reader, but to me it seems that *adbhūta* is the *angī rasa*.

The plot of any play is divisible into two main sections. The main plot is known as *adhikārika* and the related story as *prāsangika*. This latter, in its turn, is divided into two kinds, *patākā* and *prakarī*. In our play the plot of the Athenians is the main plot and there are two *prāsangika*. Both the fairies and the comic plot are *patākās* for they continue right till the very end. Prakarīs on the other hand, do not continue till the end. In this play the events that take place under the influence of the love-juice can be said to be *prakarīs*. They take the plot forward step by step but are over in a short time.

The progress of the plot has been carefully divided into several stages by Indian *ācāryas*. A detailed analysis will show how all of these can be found in our play. Here it can be mentioned that Egeus's objection to Hermia's marriage with the man of her choice is the *bīja*. In length the *nātikā* should have a minimum of five Acts and our play fulfills this requirment.

As far as the characters are concerned, the hero of a *nātikā* should be a *dhīra-lalita* hero. Here we have two romantic heroes who have not been delineated very well. The *dhīra-lalita* hero is

> Niścinto dhīra-lalitah kalāsaktah sukhī mṛduh.[14]

It has to be said that the different features of such a hero are not to be found in our two heroes mainly because we see them here as typical lovers, hardly as individuals. But we know from Egeus's description of the way in which Lysander courts Hermia that he wrote poems and songs:

> Thou hast by moonlight, at her window sung,
> With feigning voice, verses of faining love.[15]

Demetrius is almost his duplicate, so it may be assumed that he too is possessed of these accomplishments (i.e. writing songs and singing them), which were the general attributes of any young man of birth and breeding. Shakespeare has not depicted them as strongly and clearly as he has done with the other romantic heroes of his mature plays like *As You Like It* or

Twelfth Night. Both Orlando and Orsino, the heroes respectively of these two plays are ideal dhīra-lalita heroes. In this play the two romantic lovers have not been developed properly. After all, it is an early play, and Shakespeare was still learning his craft.

Theseus is not the hero, but he is an extremely important character, far better portrayed than the two lovers. Here we see him as a lover, but also as a king and he can be identified as the typical *dhirodātta* hero:

> Mahasattvo-atigambhīrah kṣamāvana-avikatthanah
> Sthiro nigūrhāṅkāro dhīrodātta dṛrhavrata.[16]

Each of these epithets can be applied, with justification, to Theseus.

When we come to the female characters, it must be remembered that there are many kinds of them in Sanskrit poetics and they have many attributes. It is difficult to classify Shakespeare's heroines as it is and here the two heroines, like the two heroes, have not been developed so well as his other heroines are. Both of them can be taken to be *madhyā-adhīrā* heroines who are outspoken in their love. They have passed beyond the shyness of first love and can speak quite openly.

A most important part of the play is the plot of the fairies. It is this that gives rise to the supremacy of *adbhūta rasa* in the play, to such an extent that the question of *aṅgī-rasa* becomes an important one. The fairies, being neither *prakhyāta* nor *utpādya*, also give rise to the question whether the play is a *nātikā* or a *prakaraṇa*. The term *prakhyāta* means something or someone (the *vastu* or the *netā*) that is concerned with the scriptures or the epics, but the fairies belong to folklore. Ācārya Dhananjaya has said:

> Atha prakaraṇe vṛtham-utpādyam loka-saṅśrayam.[17]

That is, in prakaraṇa the content is taken from folk-culture and the final outcome is the product of the poet's imagination. This is exactly what the fairies are. As a matter of fact, this play contains characters and matter of all different types, including *prakhyāta* as in Theseus, *utpādya* as in the mechanicals who are

Shakespeare's own creations, and fairies taken from folk-culture. The fairies, moreover, manipulate the plot and at the end leave a lasting impression. They suffuse the play with the kind of *adbhūta rasa* which can be classified as *divya adbhūta rasa*.

All this still does not account for the mechanicals. They are a set of charaters that are *utpādya*—created by the poet. The play is a comedy and as such should evoke *hāsya rasa*. This necessary task is done mainly by this group. These humble characters repeatedly evoke *hāsya rasa* of the *parastha* kind, and that, too, of an uncommon variety, since they themselves are not consciously making others laugh. So they are not the *āśraya* of the rasa. Instead they are the unconscious *ālambana* of it. It is only in the last scene that they become the *ālambana* with Theseus and the others as the *āśraya*. Many other rasas have been evoked in the play and a detailed analysis will reveal many beauties and complexities.

REFERENCES

1. Price, A., *op. cit.*, p. 42.
2. Wilson, John, Dover, *op. cit.*, p. 206.
3. *Ibid.*, p. 207.
4. Price, A., *op. cit.*, pp. 32-33.
5. *Ibid.*, p. 38.
6. *Ibid.*
7. Sheaight, Robert, *Granville-Barker's Production in 1914* in Price, A., *op. cit.*, p. 189.
8. Brown, John Russel, "*A Machine for Acting In*": *Peter Brook's Production of 1970,* in Price, A., *op. cit.*, p. 195.
9. Price, A., *op. cit.*, p. 25.
10. *Ibid.*, pp. 29-30.
11. *Ibid.*, p. 31.
12. Latham, Minor White, *The Elizabethan Fairies* in Price, A., *op. cit.*, p. 59.
13. Dwivedi, Hazari Prasad and Dwivedi, Prithvinatha, *Nātyasāstra ki Paramparā aur Dasarūpaka*, New Delhi, Rajkamal Prakashan, 1971, p. 67.
14. *Ibid.*, p. 113.
15. Act I, sc. i, ll. 30-31, p. 34.
16. Dwivedi *op. cit.*, p. 114.
17. *Ibid.*, p. 130.

13

Important Questions

1. Explain the significance of the title *Midsummer Night's Dream.*
2. Critically analyse the plot-structure of the play.
3. What are the dramatic strategies that Shakespeare has used in the *Dream*? How have they made the play effective?
4. Write a note on the sources that Shakespeare has used in the play and how he has coordinated them.
5. "The supreme literary merit of *A Midsummer Night's Dream* is the merit of design." Do you agree? Give reasons for your answer.
6. "In *A Midsummer Night's Dream* Shakespeare defines his characters according to what they represent." Elucidate.
7. Can Theseus be described as "the incarnation of a happy and generous rationalism?" Give reasons for your answer.
8. "Parody is the key to the only true comprehension and representation of *A Midsummer Night's Dream.*" Justify with reference to the text.
9. "Shakespeare depicts the fairies as creatures devoid of refined feelings and of morality." Do you agree?
10. "In Lysander the poet wished to represent a noble magnanimous nature." Explain with reference to the text.
11. "*A Midsummer Night's Dream* is a psychological study, not of a solitary man, but of a spirit that unites mankind." Elucidate.

12. "Bottom the weaver is the most romantic of the mechanicals." Justify.
13. "In pure poetry and the intoxication of words Shakespeare never rose higher than he rises in this play." Explain with examples from the text.
14. "*A Midsummer Night's Dream* is more of a masque than a drama—an entertainment rather than a play." Explain this statement in the light of the text.
15. "In the *Dream* the origin of love never lies in reason." Explain Shakespeare's treatment of love in this play in the light of this remark.
16. "*Pyramus and Thisbe* is but a burlesque presentment of the same theme that has occupied us." Elucidate.
17. Write a note on the imagery of the *Dream*.
18. "Shakespeare's treatment of blind love owes a good deal to mediaeval and renaissance moralisers." Elucidate.
19. Can Oberon be described as "a delicate figure for grace?" Give reasons for your answer.
20. Write a note on the poetic style of the *Dream*.

A Select Bibliography

Bradbrook, M.C., *The Growth and Structure of Elizabethan Comedies*, London, Chatto and Windus, 1955.

Brown, John Russell, *Shakespeare and His Comedies*. London Methuen, 1957.

Bullough, G., *The Narrative and Dramatic Sources of Shakespeares*, Vol. I, London, Routledge & Kegan Paul, 1957.

Champion, L.S., *The Evolution of Shakespeare's Comedies*, Harvard Univ. Press, 1973.

Charlton, H.B., *Shaksepeare's Comedies*, London, Methuen, 1977.

Clemen, W., *The Development of Shakespeare's Imagery*, London, Methuen, 1977.

Fluchére, H., *Shakespeare*, London, *Longman's* Green & Co., 1953.

Phialas, P.G., *Shakespeare's Romantic Comedies, Chapel Hill*, The Univ. of North Carolina Press, 1966.

Price, A., ed., *Shakespeare: A Midsummer Night's Dream — A Casebook*, London, Macmillan, 1983.

Ribner, I., William Shakespeare: Life Times and Theatre, New Delhi, Wiley Eastern Ltd., 1978.

Tillyard, E.M.W., *The Elizabethan World Picture*, New York, Vintage Books, No date.

Wilson, John Dover, *Shakespeare's Happy Comedies*, London Faber, paper-covered edition, No. date.

Index